Professionalism and
PRACTICE

CULTURE, VALUES and SERVICE

John Astley

The COMPANY *of* WRITERS
2006

First Published in the United Kingdom 2006
by The Company of Writers
www.thecompanyofwriters.com

© 2006 John Astley

John Astley has asserted his right under the Copyright,
Designs and Patents Act 1988.

Paperback
ISBN-(10): 0-9551834-2-1
& ISBN-(13): 978-0-9551834-2-3

British Library Cataloguing in Publication Data.
A catalogue record for this book is available from the British Library.

Classification: **Non-Fiction**
Social Sciences/Society/Work Cultures/
Professional Practice (UK)

BIC Codes
J/JB

Bibliographic Data also available:
Nielsen Book Data

Typeset in Lucida Sans

Professionalism and Practic

Collected Essays-3
John Astley

Professionalism and Practice is the third volume in John Astley's Collected Essays, which seeks to investigate aspects of the sociology of culture.

The two companion volumes are: *Liberation* and *Domestication* (which looks at youth policy in the UK); and *Culture and Creativity* (which includes essays on William Morris, Raymond Williams, and The Beatles phenomenon).

The essays in the present volume focus on culture, values and service across the spectrum of community-based professions in the United Kingdom.

The collection includes the flagship essay 'The New Professionals', which, along with the other essays, aims to examine the essentials for good, knowledge-based practice in modern professional services . . .'The University Lecturer as Research-Minded Practitioner', 'Knowledge and Practice', and 'The Quest for the Good Community' complete the sequence.

A fascinating theme emerges from the author's cumulative insights: that of 'the professions' as embattled culture groups, whose values are constantly challenged by the State and society as a whole. . .A lively debate is sure to follow any reading of these essays.

*

John Astley is a sociologist, writer, and lecturer - and a frequent contributor to journals, conferences, and radio talks. As a sociologist of culture, he is the author of three volumes of collected essays: *Liberation and Domestication, Culture and Creativity*, and *Professionalism and Practice* - as well as a celebrated monograph on The Beatles.

John Astley is currently working on *Herbivores and Carnivores*, a timely investigation into the struggle for cultural values in contemporary society.

For Finola,
A very special new professional

CONTENTS

Page

Introduction 5

The New Professionals 10

    The Sociological Context: Professions, 28
Professionals and Power

    Reflective Practice and the Reflective 46
Practitioner

    Turning the Concept of Reflective Practice 70
into Curriculum Reality

The University Lecturer as Research-Minded
Practitioner 130

Knowledge and Practice 138

The Quest for the Good Community 146

Introduction

In this, the third volume of my Collected Essays, I have brought together some writing that focuses specifically on professional cultures, and professional practice. Like the two previous volumes of essays, this one contains pieces that were written for many different purposes, but all concern themselves with my over-riding interest in the making, maintaining, changing, and breaking of culture groups and their ideas.

As a Sociologist, I have had the privilege of designing and delivering courses for a wide range of professional practitioners: nurses, midwives, youth workers, social workers, health visitors, teachers, and so on. I hope that in my engagement with this work I have adequately drawn on my role as a sociologist in a reflective way, developing my own professional practice. I have certainly seen part of my role as an attempt to apply the scope, and insights of working sociologically to help address and solve the problems of everyday life. Professional practitioners play a range of key roles that touch all our lives. This is particularly true of those practitioners involved in welfare provisions in the widest sense. For some members of society, the interventions that these practitioners make are an aspect of the significant transitions that they, as voluntary or involuntary clients, are making in their life cycle.

One sociological dimension of these everyday phenomena concerns authority and power. There can be no doubt that by dint of their role many professionals exercise power in their day-to-day inter-relationships. One of the key issues here is, of course, whether the power that professionals have is used legitimately. The different people involved in the diverse range of relationships that make up professional practice hold views on this largely dependent on the meanings placed upon the reasons for the encounters. The contextual framework within which these inter-relationships exist is an aspect of the authority issue. Sociologists know that authority = power + legitimation. Are the interventions, whatever form they take, reasonable, acceptable, needed, appropriate, welcome, or not? This is open to interpretation. However, one thing is certain here: if those on the 'receiving end' of professional interventions do not feel they are legitimate, authority will be questioned, challenged, ignored (as irrelevant), and diminished. Some people would, no doubt, be pleased by this . . !

A great deal has been written, and said (especially by politicians) concerning the empowerment of service users of all kinds. In my experience most professionals are ready and willing to promote their 'clients' as equal partners in a series of, hopefully, increasingly transparent processes that bring practice to bear on people's needs.

There are a further set of issues around the nature and use of professional bodies of knowledge, imbued as they are by research, and theory. With the empowerment of stake-holders of many kinds comes the acknowledgement that these individuals and groups have their own bodies of knowledge, which are regularly compared and contrasted with those professional ones. Expert Patients in the Health Service are just one example of this trend; there are many more, and all practitioners need to be open to the nature and role of these alternative sources of explanation, insight, and understanding. The current fashion for evidence-based practice (and workplaces) is an obvious example of where a much fuller range of knowledges impinge, intrudes, and imposes.

One fundamental aspect of policy making (who ever does it) is to deal with the present, while planning for the future. Interpretations of what has happened in the past will usually play a crucial role in shared understandings. Discussions around (collective) memory, and 'knowable communities' can play a part in these interpretations. We are all aware of the ambiguity around what constitutes past, present, and future;

and these endless speculations all contribute to the complexity of practice.

How well professionals are prepared for all this is an organising feature of these essays. 'The New Professionals' is an attempt to work through the many complex issues, and ideas, concerning the education of professional practitioners. My concern here is with both initial professional training as education, and with the educational processes that form continuing practice development. Indeed, one of the key issues addressed in this long essay is the ambiguity, and even ambivalence, around professionalisation.

There are regular events held around 'educating the workforce'. Universities are concerned enough about the (traditional) role as educators of professionals, and their recruitment targets, to offer up opportunities for discussion and debate. Many of these colleagues are only too well aware of the constant steer from the State to focus attention upon meeting various organisations workforce needs and demands. The tensions around what form the curriculum should take, whose needs it seeks to meet, and so on, is not missed by those directly engaged in devising and delivering courses. Colleagues are even compromised by these tensions, producing courses that are ill researched, and not likely to bring critically thinking, and research-minded practitioners to the competent workplace within a learning organisation.

The current literature on professionalism and practice issues is now enormous. However, a good number of the new books produced are recycling exercises that add little to either explanation or understanding. Several academic disciplines now contribute to these discussions, and inevitably many of the writers have emerged from a hybrid world of single subject disciplines and practice orientation. This is no bad thing so long as it is clear that the reader fully understands the set of values and theories that underpin the various ideas and arguments. There are always linked questions around who the audience actually is for any new books. In turn, this highlights the nature and role of research, and, for example, the values that underpin ideas of 'grassroots' respondents as the objects, or the subjects, of research. Action Research encapsulates the ideas about these issues of orientation. It is encouraging to note that more texts on professional practice, and the research that under-pins that practice, focus on these concerns, such as, 'Who is this research for?' Two very good examples of this approach are *Critical Practice in Health and Social Care*, Edited by Ann Brechin, *et al* (2000), and *Using Evidence in Health and Social Care*, Edited by Roger Gomm and Celia Davies (2000). These books specifically put the professional practitioner 'on the spot' by challenging their ideas, assumptions, and pre-paredness for practice. Do practitioners understand the provenance of the knowledge that underpins their practice? As I have indicated above, are they open to challenges to their 'authority'? All professionals should address these questions, and they should also make it their responsibility that the next generation of professionals think about them as well! This is especially true given the way that practice is increasingly 'embedded' in everyday 'community' life.

A very good recent example of such concerns is the book *Managing Community Practice* (2003) edited by Sarah Banks and colleagues. This is a wide ranging, and thoughtful collection, which overtly advocates working for the good, civil, and convivial-society values. Banks details the role of community workers, but emphasises the role played by 'a broad range of professionals, who are increasingly using community work methods in their practice'. As I write this Introduction, my involvement in the Devon Children and Young Persons (Integrated Services) Trust increases by the day. My involvement is from 'within' the voluntary youth services sector, and it is noticeable the extent to which the rhetoric of partnership and inclusiveness encounters difficulty at every stage. Strategically, and in regard to the actual funding, commissioning, procurement, provision of services, and operational issues, the statutory agencies of all professional practices are guarding their 'territory' very carefully.

Many books on professional and practice issues are now written specifically as student texts; and, while some of these authors make the origins of their ideas clear, some do not. Many of the issues around both professionalism and practice seen explicitly from a sociological perspective (even given the diversity within Sociology) tend to look quite different. As the reader will note, this is true of my own writing, where I am regularly, sooner or later, drawing on a conceptual approach that draws explicitly on ways of thinking and working sociologically.

I strive to ensure that this remains true in my work.

John Astley
Exmouth, 2006

GENERAL REFERENCES
Banks S., Butcher H., Henderson P., and Robertson J. (Editors): *Managing Community Practice,* 2003
Brechin A., Brown H., and Eby M.A., Editors: *Critical Practice in Health and Social Care,* (2000
Gomm R., and Davies C. (Editors): *Using Evidence in Health and Social Care,* 2000

The New Professionals
Reflective Practice and the Reflective Practitioner: A Critical Account

(1989)

INTRODUCTION

PRACTICE: CONTEXT, CONDITIONS AND CARE

This essay is concerned with the concept of reflective practice and the possibility of designing and delivering a curriculum for professionals that realises their potential as reflective practitioners.

The essay itself is intended to be a piece of reflective practice and my methodology is that of a 'critical theorist' within sociology in that what follows is essentially a piece of theoretical analysis. A good deal of my essay does, however, identify questions that could be pursued by empirical research methods. My own brand of sociology typically creates far more questions than I can personally take up in field work research, but I do have intentions to pursue some research avenues beyond this essay and possibly the essay itself will generate sufficient interest among some readers in that they may take up the challenge of research.

The context of this essay is a concern I have with health care practitioners and the educational processes whereby they become accepted and qualified members of their professions. However, there is a broader context in which this essay is set, that of the professional education of 'people-workers' in more general terms. For example, my involvement with social work courses, youth and community work courses, and teacher education has given me an interest in seeing the generality of issues at a curriculum design and delivery level.

My interest in the education of 'people-workers' in general, and (in this essay) health care practitioners in particular, is also motivated by my interest in the morality of these occupations. It seems to me that these professions in particular claim a special status on the basis of their virtuous ideas and actions. It is difficult to deny that these professions are vital to the welfare of our populations and that given the criteria available for what might be considered a worthy occupation and vocation, these practitioners can argue for special status. What attracts women and men to nursing is to give service through care and this motivation seems little changed in the last twenty years since McGuire (1969). On the question of virtue, see *After Virtue*, MacIntyre (1981).

It would seem that given most debates about what constitutes basic human needs, a focus on welfare is still regarded with high priority in our society. A number of recent pieces of sociological research indicate that, despite the many changes to official welfare and/or social security policy in Britain in recent years, there remains a significant commitment by the public to welfare and caring (Walker, A. and Westergaard, J., 1988, Gallie, D., 1989).

Indeed it is justifiably argued that devotion to welfare is still seen as part of the civilizing process in our society. Despite many pressures to relinquish this collectivist commitment in favour of a set of selfish goals, our population appears to be resilient in maintaining their hold on these values.

In this Introduction, I would like to consider these observations at more length in relation to a concern with the interrelationship between knowledge and human interests. Before doing that though, I would like to offer a brief account of my growing self-consciousness about reflective practice.

I first came across the notion of reflective practice in relation to teacher education. Whether by accident or design, I recall reading *Knowledge and Control*, a series of essays on the sociology of education edited by Michael F. D. Young, shortly after the book's publication in 1971. I am surely not

11

alone in the thought-provoking effect that those essays, as a collection, had on my consciousness. Having very cautiously entered into the world of formal education from my background in sociology, my sensibilities were being teased by the prospect of embarking on teaching. Reading that book gave me some insight into the real difficulties that faced me as a sociologist, attempting to bring my 'sociological imagination', my critical reflexiveness, to a teaching role and the contradictions arising in that role. *That* knowledge certainly confirmed for me a growing sense of my own limitations. Not so much perhaps in my ability to transmit certain bodies of 'sociological' knowledge in an entertaining and thoughtful way, more so perhaps my limitations in what I was prepared to do with the insights I gained about my new role.

In short, was I prepared to get down off my academic pedestal, deconstruct my role *vis-à-vis* my discipline, re-examine my relationships, expose my reciprocity to the 'acid test' of real democratic thought and practice? Would I be able to learn from my practice while helping others to learn from theirs, while performing the role, and giving of service, as was expected of me?

What was also important for me was that I was not merely considering epistemological questions, but actually focusing upon questions of agency.

> "The development of a reflexive sociology, in sum, requires that sociologists cease acting as if they thought of subjects and objects, sociologists who study and 'laymen' who are studied, as two different breeds of men. There is only one breed of man. But so long as we are without a reflexive sociology, we will act upon the tacit dualistic premise that there are two regardless of how monistic our professions of methodological faith.

> I conceive of reflexive sociology as requiring an empirical dimension which might foster a large variety of researches about sociology and sociologists in their occupational roles, their career 'hang-ups', their establishments, power systems, sub-cultures and their place in the larger social world."
>
> *(Gouldner, 1971, p.490/1)*

While being aware of a certain gender-sensitivity here, I would endorse Gouldner's view.

These concerns have remained with me over many years of teaching and I shall attempt to share these with the reader.

I make no apologies for the nature of what follows. Despite my rigour as a sociologist engaged constantly in researching the real world, a good deal of what follows is much like a philosophical meditation.

Let me now return, as promised, to outline some of the concerns that brought me to write an essay called 'The New Professionals'.

Not surprisingly, the tidal wave of demands for a 'return to market forces' has even buffeted the safe havens of the professions. A good deal of rhetoric has been expended in the last decade or so on the overwhelming need for professionals to reassess their role in terms of the new enterprise culture environment.

> "The professions face unprecedented chall-enges as, increasingly, the question is asked: can they survive in their present form? Lord MacKay's proposed reforms of the legal profession show the Government is not afraid to take a well-entrenched group by the scruff

13

of the neck to protect the consumer against restrictive practices.

Professionals and their associations are wrestling with such issues as multi-disciplinary practice - in which members of differing professions work together in one business - and whether firms should be allowed to incorporate with limited liability.

Customers in the marketplace are adopting a more robust attitude towards suppliers of professional services. New patterns of work are emerging, while information technology and the prospect of a single European market pose challenges and present opportunities.

For the first time in decades, the question is being asked: Is a learned professional necessarily competent? The Training Agency and the National Council for Vocational Qualifications are seeking out new opportunities to define and package competencies.

The professional marketplace is becoming more competitive, with the result that the professional may no longer be king. Customer power is growing and fee scales are being questioned. Clients seem more willing to seek legal redress and the cost of professional indemnity cover is soaring. The words relevance, quality and price occur more frequently at review meetings.

Market performance is likely to be the acid test in selecting those to run professional practices and professional institutes. Lifetime loyalty and lifetime membership should no longer be assumed.

> Professional firms and professional inst-
> itutes may need to become less like local
> authorities and more like go-getting com-
> panies. Functional bureaucracy may have to
> give way to flexibility and team working."

(Coulson-Thomas, 1989)

This is a lengthy quote but it serves my purpose very well as it catches exactly the mood of the decade. Although many professionals in the public sector, in general, and health care practice in particular, may have felt some years ago that the issues raised here were not going to touch them, matters have rapidly changed. The technical rationality and 'new' managerialist approaches of public sector bureaucracies have made significant inroads into organisation and working practices. Taking their lead from government, more and more bureaucrats have adopted a set of operational attitudes that have taken many professional practitioners by surprise. In this essay I have devoted some considerable space to an account of the professions and do not therefore intend a lengthy exposition here. However, I signal these issues because if I am to debate the strengths and weaknesses of the development of reflective practice amongst professional practitioners it is essential to locate this debate in the context of significant change.

One of the key issues that has to be addressed is the question of purpose in engaging in reflective practice. What is it for? Is it to make for a more enlightened and insightful individual practitioner? Is it to focus attention upon the relation between the practitioner as subject and the practice, care, client relations as object? Is it to raise the level of consciousness about practice as a consequence of, and with the intention of, changing the nature of, care giving?

There are undoubtedly considerable contradictions asso-ciated with all of these motivation scenarios, not the least of which is the possibility, even if desired, of becoming a more insightful professional practitioner without becoming in oneself a living critique of the social-organisational order within which that practice takes place.

Consciousness raising and practice changing may well be seen to go hand in hand, but this has implications for change, both personal and social. There is no doubt at all that reflective practice - reflection in action and praxis are seen as (the most) significant vehicles for the psychological development of the individual.

It is absolutely essential to address what I would call the conditions of practice. Under what set of circumstances, including change, can practice take place? We are not merely concerned with content, which may seem to be the motive for curriculum innovation, but form. What structures of practice paradigms are merging? How will the roles that go to make up these structures be formed?

The changes that subject and object consciousness bring about, or seek to bring about, provide the 'space' for renegotiation of role(s). However, it is also necessary to recognise and emphasise the importance of collective action in the interrelation between consciousness, practice and change.

Part of this collective action might well be educational in both intent and outcome. Those of us who are engaged in the development of educational programmes, who spend time devising and speculating upon pedagogic strategies should certainly be aware of this concern with *collective action*. If we are to treat each student as an island, as a *totally* autonomous personality, we would possibly lay foundations for that student to become a very limited reflective practitioner.

If the economic, social and political conditions on which the whole *process of individualisation* depends do not offer a basis for the realisation of individuality, while at the same time people have lost those ties that gave them security, this lag makes freedom an unbearable burden. Powerful tendencies arise to escape from this kind of freedom into submission of some kind of relationship to people and the world, which promises relief from uncertainty, even if it deprives the individual of freedom. This has resonances in the changed/changing situation of the working class since 1945 - and is especially true for each younger generation since the war - increasingly '*liberated*' from existing bounds of culture and society, but not in fact given the means to realise their individuality.

I would argue that this is especially so for a whole spectrum of professionals including health care practitioners. There are real dangers in setting up educational scenarios in which nurses, social workers, teachers, *etc.,* are told they must be, are, a certain kind of professional practitioner, while the conditions of practice both 'inside' and 'outside' of their courses do not support this.

This whole issue is related to the relation between and contradiction of social character and the productive ideal located in society today. The pursuit of either in an uncritical and unreflective way spells danger. If we are to argue that reflective practice is a/the way to develop the social character and that the occupational/productive ideal is to be a carer - we must recognise the dangers in isolating these two and attempting to pursue them independently.

In this context I am asking, can we educate professionals not to be like most professionals presently are? What needs to be done to select and prepare appropriate role models for our students? Can we equip professionals with the skills to gain insights into self and society-social structures that can lead them to be free to take action that will create the conditions of practice that will lead to the 'good society'? I would cite Habermas as an exemplary illustration of those writers arguing that any debate about professional knowledge must be seen within the context of human interests. (Habermas, 1978).

Professionals have traditionally been given freedom *from*, because of the lesser degree of alienation they are supposed to have experienced. Can they turn this advantage into freedom *to*?

Paul Halmos is typical of many writers attempting to address these contradictions. He draws on C. Wright Mills' *Sociological Imagination* in seeing the personal/political dichotomy as an aspect of his concern about *change-agents*. Every citizen is a change-agent argues Halmos, but do they *realise* it? He argues that there remains a need to raise consciousness to this effect. Halmos is interested in the extent to which 'personalist-workers' (what I would call people-workers) are concerned with the *whole* of a client and how this 'personalist' approach contrasts with a political approach.

Halmos offers what he calls an equilibrist position, the desire to maintain an effective interrelation between, often apparently, opposites, 'logically incompatible positions'. Halmos argues that this is what Gouldner refers to as a reflexive sociology.

> "...the equilibrator works in doubt and with inadequate knowledge, but this will prompt him to explore and respond to the puzzling facts."
>
> *(Halmos, 1978, p.171)*

Halmos argues, *à la* Mills, that personal troubles cannot be solved merely *as troubles* but must be understood in terms of public issues and in terms of the problems of history making.

Halmos, like many other professional practitioners and commentators on same, reiterates the 'cult of uncertainty'. He locates his ambivalence within the two dominant traditions of 'people-working' in post-war Britain, namely, social democratic reformism and psychoanalytic therapy. But will these do now? Is human misery, poverty and despair a result of personal inadequacy or social injustice? Is the solution, therefore, to these problems confronted by professional practitioners, psychotherapy - or political action? The conflict between a desire to help those in need and a fear that, by doing so, they support an unacceptable political system is at the heart of a heartless world for many professional practitioners.

Some observers would be more critical than Halmos. Narr, for example, argues that the 'welfare state' has always been an expression of crisis and not its solution. (Narr, 1969). Heller, as a neo-Marxist, would not support any view that all human needs can be supplied in the marketplace. (Heller, 1976). This certainly relates to the context and role of caring. Can care to be produced and sold/consumed in the marketplace, with competition and profit, personal and corporate accumulation of wealth and/or power as attendant factors? Do not the characteristics of supply and demand focused on market mechanisms actually have a tendency to distort the nature of care relationships? The price of everything and the value of nothing!

It is quite clear that arguments about good practice focus on consciousness-raising as action aimed at social change. Peter Leonard has argued that there are essentially two models of practice, that which is action-orientated and that which is consciousness-orientated.

> "The first, *action-orientated practice*, lays great emphasis on the achievement of material changes through collective action. Focus centres on the common material interests and concerns of those involved and the practical means by which material improvements can be obtained. The process of identifying and realising common material interests may lead to such changes in

19

consciousness as are likely to accompany the necessity for moving from narrow individualism to some conception of collective needs. Within this form of practice, substantial changes in consciousness are a possible outcome, but are not a primary objective of the practice. Much trade union activity can be seen as an example of practice, which does not aim primarily to develop a critical consciousness of an oppressive social order, but to gain material benefits for its members. Those living on social security benefits who organised themselves into Claimants Unions placed more emphasis than trade unions do on developing overall critiques of the social order which ensured their poverty, but still identified their starting point as the practical struggle for improved state benefits.

The second, *consciousness-oriented practice*, although it sees practical action as an outcome, places its initial emphasis on the changes in consciousnesses that are necessary before effective action can take place. Here, understanding of oneself in the context of the social order is the first priority, rather than the immediate identification of (possibly superficial) material interests. Women's consciousness-raising groups, and those men's groups which are concerned with combating gender oppression, are prime examples of this kind of practice."

(Leonard, 1984, p.209/210)

Leonard is reminding us that these models pose differences in ideas about whether the material conditions of everyday life or ideology constitute the really significant element in shaping what I have called the conditions of practice, which may, or may not, be changing over time.

These dilemmas for actual or potential professional practitioners are consistently pointed to by reflective professional educators; often in quite unassuming ways. For example, David Neal in his remarks on the organisation of a 'relevant' curriculum for sociology on CQSW courses says:

> "Of what possible use could sociology be to social workers or to their clients? Will it explain 'the family I visit down the road'? What differences exist between sociology and other 'social sciences'? Is it just an arbitrary division of labour? What can a history of sociology tell us about doing sociology? What type of sociology/social work is being discussed above? Are there certain types of sociology for certain types of social work? If so, why? What notion of 'society' is used in different types of sociology and by different kinds of social workers? Are social workers their own sociologists? Should they be? *Can they afford to be*? What type of sociology teaching would promote or hinder this?"
>
> [My emphasis].

(Neal in Gomm and McNeil, 1982, p.279)

Similarly, David Armstrong is here discussing his approach to teaching sociology at Guy's Hospital Medical School, and specifically his concern with the effective aspects of the curriculum.

21

"Karl Popper is reputed to have asked his class on the first day of his course, "Tell me what you can see." The students replied, "What should we be looking at?" There is now considerable evidence from sources as varied as the sociology of science to basic cognitive processes that people do not 'see' in a vacuum, but bring to situations particular mental sets or frameworks which ultimately determine what they are.

The architect sees a structure, where the engineers see stresses and the layman sees a home.

The problem that these mental frameworks present for the sociology teacher is that students come to their subject with a far more sophisticated and developed mental set than they do to anatomy or biochemistry, simply because they know more about society having lived in it. A critical part of a medical sociology course therefore inevitably involves challenging pre-established beliefs, even though this can often be seen as threatening by faculty or students. However, the emphasis is on challenging rather than changing beliefs: effective change, consolidation or confusion all seem acceptable as long as alternatives have been considered."

(Armstrong in Gomm and McNeill, 1982, p.285)

These very practical curricular concerns do rest upon concerns about well-being, about welfare, about care. They touch on the attempt through practice to connect with real people and not theoretical abstractions. This concern is certainly a focus of most modernist thought, the reuniting of human beings and their environment. These debates have often centred on seeing human agency for change in collective as well as individualistic terms. Gramsci's work on hegemony is an obvious example.

> "Gramsci sees the possibility of changing the very objects of social enquiry, assumed as fixed by Bukharin, through 'working up' those beliefs within an organisation which effectively constructs a socialised, less particularistic objectivity in practice."

> *(Kilminster, 1979, p.245)*

Major shifts have taken place over recent years in the foci of attention and action for people-workers. We have witnessed an increased concern with identifying with and responding to, the 'whole person'. Clients, patients, whatever, have become less of a collection of objective fragments and more of an inter-subjective agent for personal change.

Including clients/patients within their action assessment, practitioners have increasingly embraced the notion that human attributes are the produce of training and practice and that they depend for their maintenance on use.

Hirst and Woolley have argued that important though social relations and culture are in our understanding of human attributes, we should not exclude some reference to biological and psychological influences (Hirst and Woolley, 1982). They cite Levi-Strauss' argument that no empirical analysis can determine the point of transition between natural and cultural facts, nor how they are connected. Levi-Strauss shows a healthy scepticism about the possibility of an empirical differentiation between nature and culture on the grounds that we can find no pre-social state in the

23

evaluation of the human species and because there is no clear way of assigning attributes exclusively to natural causes or to social conditions.

What we see coming together as concerns are elements of the condition(s) of practice, both of the self and of the social.

Travelbee argues that professional education leads to the development of a 'nursing conscience' resulting from absorption by the nursing student of a certain belief and value system (Smith, 1981). Smith himself suggests that this is the professional ethic of collective conscience and in cultural terms is what Bernstein would call part of the sentiment of the group.

One of my key concerns throughout this essay is to ask whether nurses, and other 'people-workers', develop, are guided or coached to develop, a human-relations model for their practice.

It is not surprising, therefore, that a good deal of the evidence I consider in this essay concerns organisational behaviour. One of the aspects of the aim to develop reflective practice that I discuss below is precisely that nature of the social and cultural environment of the learner and the teacher, and the *learning* and the *teaching*.

One dimension of my discussions on the conditions of practice and developing reflective practice is, therefore, focused on organisational factors. Are they liberating and enabling or domesticating and alienating?

Argyris suggests that the needs of formal organisations prevent the needs of healthy individuals and that job or role enlargement and enrichment, and employee-centred leadership will not tend to work to the extent necessary. He argues that those persons that manage the organisation can only effectively lead (and give leadership) by dealing with the reality of the organisation. They require to be informed and remain informed (Argyris, 1957). I argue that unless the curriculum designers and deliverers approach these contextual matters openly, their naivety will prevent adequate development of reflective practice. Teachers as well as learners must include their course, curriculum, organisation style, *etc.* within their conceptualisation of developing reflective practice. Being a reflective practitioner cannot exist in a vacuum.

Most devotees of reflective practice argue that it can be taught, that it is certainly caught, but must also acknowledge that it can be fraught!

McEvoy is just one writer who has recently expressed fears about the gap between reforming rhetoric and actual delivery.

> "One major anxiety surrounding Project 2000 concerns the quality of the clinical learning experiences which will be offered to the new 'species' of student. Under Project 2000 it is envisaged that students will spend at least 50% of their training time in a clinical environment where they will gradually make a contribution to care, under the mentorship of a named qualified nurse. Obviously careful and consistent monitoring of the clinical learning environment will be crucial; and this should begin now.
>
> At present, nurse educators monitor the clinical learning environment through student and tutor learning evaluations. But it is difficult to assess a clinical area as a profitable educational experience for students when those same students make a substantial contribution to the nursing service.
>
> Under Project 2000 this situation will change and we must be ready to take full advantage of a whole new ball game. We must courageously grade clinical areas according to the quality of the learning experiences that they

propose to offer. To protect the morale of clinical staff this must be done sensitively, but nonetheless rigorously. Selecting the appropriate methods and approach will be critical. Even if a clinical area has to be rejected, this can be done with tact and courtesy using criteria, which will provide guidance to raising standards for care and learning...

The process of confronting and addressing the quality of clinical experience will create stress for everyone. But the stress will be much worse if the problems have not been resolved before the first flow of supernumerary students arrives with expectations that cannot be fulfilled. Attempting the impossible is not a good strategy; it is just a waste of resources. As we continue to monitor these learning environments we must not be misled by superficial appearances or the diplomacy of clinical managers. Enhancement of the clinical learning environment will require considerable effort, at times be inconvenient, and even disrupt traditional attitudes and practices."

(McEvoy, 1989)

I could easily fill many pages with salutary tales of innovations that have foundered. If reflective practice is to be developed as a key and core aspect of education for professional practice then a good deal more than fine words will be required.

What follows in this essay is an attempt to further set the context, to say more about the nature of the professions in our society, to describe and discuss the concept of reflective practice and to tentatively outline some problems associated with turning the idea of developing reflective practice into curriculum reality. I trust I have left the reader with some speculations and evidence on which to make an assessment or judgement about the viability of the project of developing more human beings into reflective practitioners, the new professionals.

The Sociological Context: Professions, Professionals and Power

What follows is by no means an exhaustive account of the commentary on professions made by sociologists. I merely intend this to be an indication of relevant debates.

THE GROWTH OF PROFESSIONS

Although professional workers existed before the early nineteenth century, it was the rapid process of industrialisation, with rationalisation, specialisation of production and intensified division of labour that created the situation where so-called professional workers have become an integral part of society. There are some well-known attempts to rationalise the growth of professions. Are there common characteristics that could help to qualify or disqualify occupational groups? Millerson (1964) in his study, developed six traits of the 'model' profession:

1. A skill based on theoretical knowledge
2. An extensive period of education
3. The testing of competence before admission to the profession
4. The existence of a code of conduct
5. A theme of public service
6. The freedom of the profession to regulate itself.

Professionalisation has been complementary to the process whereby occupation has become the typical basis of differentiation in society. Jencks in the USA, and Boudon in France, have been typical of sociologists who have stressed the rise of the 'meritocratic' society, where educational success is increasingly valued as the means of achieving the end of access to such high-status occupations as the professions. Many occupational groups aspiring to professional status have sought to use educational achievement as the lever to elevate them to a higher rung in the occupational hierarchy. This process of professionalisation has been further accelerated by an increasingly democratic society. It is interesting and often paradoxical that the late 19th and 20th century demands for social reforms, which have created extensive welfare provision and a public service sector, brought about the conditions for the rapid growth of professional occupations. The increase in the size of the professions and the number of professional occupations was augmented by other changes in post-War British society, such as the reforms in secondary education. These reforms gave a limited access to professional work to people otherwise excluded by lack of acceptable social background, and/or education. Many of the boys and girls of the upper working class, were able to move in socially mobile ways into occupations, rewards, conditions and status that their parents could not have enjoyed (Jackson & Marsden, 1962).

Movement took place into 'white-collar', and often public sector, jobs. However, it might be argued that a good deal of this movement was intra, rather than inter, class.

Service industries especially have expanded in the last thirty years in Britain or elsewhere. The state's intervention in the Economy, and increasingly in the everyday lives of citizens, has meant the creation of jobs that have, in turn, been filled by aspiring professionals, newly educationally accredited, to fill such occupational roles.

PROFESSIONALISATION AND SOCIAL MOBILITY

Education and paper qualifications have increasingly become the arbiter of someone's fitness for access to a professional occupation (Young, 1958, Jackson & Marsden, 1962). However, it would be injudicious to over-estimate the degree of even upper-working class access to the professions. Goldthorpe's study (1979) emphasises the limited nature of access to what he calls the 'service-class' - people with well-paid jobs with career prospects in the professions. The 1979

Nuffield surveys indicate that men born between 1908 and 1917 and brought up between the wars in working-class families had a 14% chance of reaching the 'service-class'.

For men born to similar families between 1938 and 1947, the chance had risen to 18%. However, the study also shows that those men born into such professional families in the 1938-47 period had an even greater prospect of achieving access to a professional occupation to the 1908-17 generation. This study would seem to suggest that ascribed status is still a distinctive feature of post-war Britain.

PROFESSIONS AND ELITES

One important feature of professionalisation in the last hundred years has been the extent to which this occupational group, wide as it is, has come to be dominant as advisers to the State, local government, business management and the like. Whether we look at commerce, the law, medicine, government or the 'people-work' or management professions like healthcare, teaching, welfare and social services, does not seem to make much difference. Professionals have often, it seems, come to be the 'hand-maidens' of the development of industrial capitalist society and socialist industrial societies alike.

It is perhaps not surprising, therefore, that sociologists have come to ask questions about the role of professions as exclusive, virtually self-perpetuating elites in society; taking on and developing, perhaps, the characteristics of bureaucratic organisations central to the everyday management of society. Professionals have also, most importantly, been essential to the planning and policy-making processes within these dominating institutions of society. They have, as the facilitators of progress and technocrats of advanced industrial society, been in a position to shape the development of society very much in their own way. Although professionals are a small proportion of the total labour force in any industrial society they exert influence and control over the lives, rights and activities of many other workers. The autonomy and control of the professions may have been challenged in the last decade, but their indelible mark remains on our social structure.

Professionals have also often come to be, and to be seen as, the definers of the nature of social relations and human behaviour. Professionals *profess*; and in so doing create knowledge of a valued kind (Hughes, 63).

> "Routine definitions of ill-health, social adequacy, school achievement, degrees of criminality, for example, can be seen as grounded in the specific forms of expertness which at any one time are dominant categories of thought which permeate over commonsense attitudes - as well as the power to enforce them - and are to some extent traceable to the political organisation of particular occupations, *e.g.* the judiciary, psychiatry and social work. Perhaps more important is the fact that professional legitimacy is often so strongly embedded and taken for granted that the cognitive frame-works within which we think about various social issues appear entirely self-evident and rational. Indeed, by appealing to a kind of universality and value neutrality in their knowledge, the professions put it in a sense beyond the social structures in which it has been formulated. In this way they portray a highly political process as non-political."

(Esland, 1977, p.84)

PROFESSIONS AND IDEOLOGY

The growth and increasing power of secular knowledges is a major factor in the modernisation processes. I mention this here because a good deal of what I want to argue in relation

31

to the possible, likely or actual changes in the professions focuses attention upon the contradictions of the place of the professions in modern society. In *Facing up to Modernity*, Peter Berger comments on this issue.

> "In the contemporary world (this) dynamic of modernisation/counter-modernisation is readily visible. There continues to be aggressive ideologies of modernity, confidently asserting that the *transformations* of our age are the birth pangs of a better life for humanity."
>
> *(Berger, 1979, p.102)*

Professional ideologies are most certainly contemporary examples of this assertive modernity. Some of the central features of this dynamic that Berger refers to in *Facing up to Modernity* is 'individuation'.

> "Modernisation has entailed a progressive separation of the individual from collective entities and as a result has brought about a historically unprecedented counter position of individual and society. This individuation is, as it were, the other side of the coin of... abstraction."
>
> *(Berger op. cit. p.106)*

For Berger this individuation runs contrary to the best interest of social welfare or wellbeing. One of the issues raised by this section of my essay is the emphasis placed upon individual freedoms, operational autonomies and discretionary powers experienced and enjoyed by most professionals, which need to be addressed in any critical account of the professions and the likelihood of change. The acculturation process for most professionals actually inculcates and celebrates the (relative) autonomy of the professional.

In this sense, professions and professionals are seen as a major source of ideology production; creating the dominant ideas of and about society, and of and about themselves as essential to society.

Professionals have often been discussed in terms of their 'gate-keeper' role in the distribution of industrial societies' scarce resources. They have, after all, seemed in their role as experts to be the most appropriate people to make rational decisions about the distribution of scarce resources, human or material. The bureaucratic institutions that professionals have helped to create in the last hundred years have confirmed and reconfirmed the necessary roles of such experts of corporate management. I do not doubt that social scientists, including sociologists, have often been an integral part of this process. The writing of Mills (1959), O'Neill (1972), Gouldner (1971) or Bauman (1976), would all support the idea that sociology must be accountable and reflexive and that essentially sociology is a symbiotic science-profession whose promise is to give back to society an enhanced version of what it takes from them.

There are, however, contradictions inherent in any such social development, and it is so here.

In this respect, the role of the professional is essentially political. Politics is about resources. It is about the allocation of resources and the decisions about allocation. It is about how power comes to be more the province of some individuals and social groups than of others and how this fact affects resources. As social theorists, we are concerned with the social basis of politics, with, for example, how it is that some individuals or groups come to have more decision-making power than others. What is the history of these unequal relations? What forces are at work that seek or serve to maintain or change these situations? However, we can no longer just talk in conventional and traditional terms of the individual or of social class. We live in a time of bureaucratic organisations, some of which administer 'welfare'. Even when the government is dramatically changing the role of State Institutions the influence of these bureaucracies can be felt. Part of this change is an increasing split between bureaucratic and professional motivations, values, means and ends. What follows is an attempt to examine the nature and consequences of this split.

We have, within our welfare institutions, professional values, roles and personnel that have been brought about by modernising and often humanitarian forces-factors. These institutions are some of the 'sites of struggles', 'battle-grounds', for certain kinds of social change set against attempts to resist many such changes. We are also centrally concerned with the power these institutions have to make and shape ideas about decisions, about resources and their allocation. We are concerned to understand the relationship between bureaucratic and professional ideas, practice and authority in these institutions.

One aspect of our interest and concern in this bureaucratic-professional split is that it was not always so self-consciously evident to the professionals themselves. In the first flush of development the institutional roles of social welfare provision, in the widest sense, were seen as good and positive - a clear moral posture embracing a set of ideas that reckoned the outcomes of these welfare interventions to be worth the administrative complexities. Less emphasis was placed on the organisational means than on the ends. The bureaucratic and professional were virtually collapsed together. In the last twenty years or so, the administrative process has become much more a significant issue: means have come to be the focus just as much as ends. Now this may be because professionals love to profess. As people have taken on professional roles they have 'fleshed them out' and made them much more 'a thing in themselves'.

However, it is important in these debates to acknowledge the arguments of those social theorists who see a distinctive difference between the traditional professions and the newer 'people-workers'. Bennett & Hockenstad, for example, argue that in two key respects, knowledge base and autonomy, the 'people-workers' are different. Firstly, the knowledge base is more derived from, and interrelated with, practice and the necessary skills developed by practitioners. These practice knowledges are seen by practitioner and client alike as a different kind of authority, an authority derived from the very service, which is given in a more democratic relation. Secondly, most 'people-workers' have been heirs to the social institutions developed by statutory and voluntary organisations since 1945. They are professional and yes, almost by definition, they are not self-employed, auto-nomous workers, they are employed by agencies of health and social services, education, *etc.*

Not surprisingly, therefore, this line of argument goes some way towards an explanation of contradictions and conflicts that arise as a consequence of different inter-pretations of roles, means and ends between 'people-workers' and those that employ, administer or manage them (Bennett, W. S. and Hockenstad, M. C. in Halmos, 1973).

PROFESSIONS AND VESTED INTERESTS

We come back to a fundamental question. On whose behalf do the professions operate? Are they, in the pluralist's terms, merely carrying out a series of functions on behalf of society as a whole, the occupiers of these professional roles having been suitably 'qualified' to do so. Or are they, in the elitist theorist's terms, an inevitability of human social organ-isation, i.e. given any conglomeration of human beings, a few very significant organisers will always emerge as the appropriate facilitators of order? Or again, in the Marxist's terms, are they the well-paid lackeys of the ruling class (or ruling elite of Russia, say) who have the degree of autonomy allowed them by the real economic and political rulers of society?

In terms of work and working, the role of professionals in manufacturing and service industries has become increasingly significant.

Sociologists of industry have turned their attention to, *e.g.* the role of personnel managers, or as Tony Watson (1977) has called them, 'the people-processors'. Watson, like Halmos (1970), has emphasised the important nature of this professional group's role as the providers of labour of suitable calibre. In the right place at the right time. These professionals are required to provide as rationally and cost-effectively as demanded, the appropriate units of labour power and yet, at one and the same time, need to keep themselves aware of the desires, needs and wants of workers of all kinds, including fellow professionals.

This group of aspiring professionals also reflect an important concern for sociologists of professions, namely the development and influence of the professional association. Whether we be talking of the British Medical Association or the Institute of Personnel Management or the RCN, it is possible to observe the 'gatekeeping' and regulatory function of such professional associations. These associations have invariably been dubbed the 'trade unions' of the professions, and there are some points of similarity in that the origins of both types of organisation can be seen to be derived from the medieval guild system, with its setting of standards for access, role as training agent, arbiter of general rules of conduct and facilitator of improved status, pay and conditions for its membership.

There is constantly a contradiction present between the professional as an individual - well educated, powerful and perhaps with a sophisticated lifestyle - and the professional as a member of an organisation, perhaps a bureaucracy. Sociologists have disagreed as to the extent that the authority claimed by and given to professions and professionals is based on rational criteria. Are they the most suitable people to make judgements about important features of others' likes? The professions themselves have invariably emphasised their necessarily exclusive and expert role, but many professionals may, in practice, find it difficult to make choices between the ethos and rules of conduct of their chosen profession, and the demands of the organisation that they work for. Many professionals do, for example, deliberately make public, issues that the organisation they work for has considered best kept secret. This cannot only cause conflict for the professionals themselves, but can cause conflicts in the organisational or societal sphere as well. Peter Worsley has suggested that the role of 'professional' will tend to differ in societies where an underlying individualistic philosophy of possessive property ownership is 'replaced' by a collective response to social needs. This can be noted in societies like China or Mexico or Tanzania, where mass medical services are provided by large numbers of rudimentarily trained medical staff to supplement the existing core of highly qualified, temporarily scarce, professionals (Worsley, 1977).

We must not assume that because some sociologists have identified and discussed what they consider to be the dominance of professions and professionals, and that the professionals themselves often value highly their contribution, that the majority of people recognise or accept this.

Johnson (1972) has emphasised this aspect of the debate on professionals in discussing 'trait' theory. This is the way in which many sociologists have drawn up a list of prominent functions of professions and professionals which is seen to outline their role and thereby their importance to progress and stability in society.

As Johnson points out, this has tended to take the existence of professionals, as an aspect of the division of labour and differentiation in society, for granted. It is a view that has tended to reinforce and even legitimate the professionals as an elite within an increasingly plural social order, without, in fact, raising the question of the nature, and distribution of, economic and political power in society.

I would, however, want to add a note of caution in the ongoing debate about the professions, professionals and power. The last twenty years has seen considerable arguments presented by the likes of Illich, Braverman and Foucault on the power of the professions located in their knowledge base. Foucault and the other 'deprofessionalisers' have offered an influential panoptic view of professions arguing a tyrannical homogenous disciplinary apparatus. The work of Freidson, for example, has offered a consistently sceptical view. While acknowledging the profound changes that have taken place in industrial societies in relation to the professions, Friedson, like Bucher and Strauss, places much more emphasis upon the structural sources of diversity, dissent and occupational segmentation. Freidson argues that it is real individual human beings that are the reservoirs, the embodiment of knowledge and that these people are sustained by organised institutions. Freidson therefore places much less significance on 'self-employment' among the professions (Illich 1977, Braverman 1974, Foucault 1974, Freidson 1971 and 1988, Bucher and Strauss 1961).

It may be one project to 'de-professionalise' society; can we envisage a society without professionals in their present form? It is perhaps another project to seek to 'de-ideologise' the professions? Whether this is desirable or practical is one set of questions. Whatever view was expressed here, some notice would have to be taken of how it would be done. Would professional education, pre- or in-service be the best hope? However, with the apparently unlimited enthusiasm of occupational groups and individuals to achieve professional status, is it likely that any counter policy to remove the symbolic and practical boundaries of these occupational cultures would stand much chance of success?

It is somewhat ironic if we have to wait for groups or individuals to become status conscious professionals before they look to argue against the weaknesses of their isolated position, or the very existence of professions in society. One other glaring example of inconsistency can be added. Many professions offer examples of the ideological imbalance of other professions. Many professions and professionals offer formal and informal critiques of other professions and professionals. They rarely turn that critique or analysis on themselves. Indeed, part and parcel of the endless social reproduction of social relations in our societies and the re-legitimation that certain groups achieve, is precisely because they so assiduously seek it!

I have already referred, in this section of my essay, to the 'problems' or contradictions associated with individuation or the distinctive ideas about autonomy that most profess-ionals have. Before progressing it is necessary to identify some of the concerns that sociologists and other social theorists have expressed about this facet of modern life and attempts to understand it.

It is not at all unusual to see sociologists stating their belief in the 'self-society tension' concept derived essentially from the work of C. Wright Mills (1959). This analytical tool (having the sociological imagination to see it, have insight into it, and with it) has often been slightly reformulated as the concept of the dialectical relationship between society and individuals.

But what are these interrelations? Of what separable components/factors/variables are they composed? If there is a balance or balances to be struck between them, where does it lie? Which, for example, are the most significant factors to consider? Not the least important reason for wanting to know this would be in policy and social-personal change and development terms. Will the most significant factors for one person or group be the same for everyone? From what research has been done on ascribed and achieved status, life chances, *etc.*, it would seem very unlikely that everyone is the same for analytical purposes. Can we measure, account for and explain these various and varying factors using the same techniques of sociological analysis? Do we expect the outcomes to be the same if we argue that the inputs, even given patterns of similarity, are very different?

Culture(s) provide us with a further set of difficulties. Culture is traditionally used by sociologists to recognise how human beings, individually and/or collectively, resolve the contradictions of self-society. We are here moving into analytical terrain where meaning seems to become a much more significant aspect of our speculations. Not the least of concerns here is the extent to which human beings, individually and/or collectively take action in their reflection upon their situation (praxis). What is also significant here is the importance placed upon the concept of *role* in situating both ideas and material existence in the life course and chances of human beings.

The debate about meaning and ideas is crucial in any analysis of society and self. Certainly a good deal has been said over the years about which factors of any person's life is more determining, the material conditions of their everyday lives (and the relationships that are part and parcel of that) or the ideas that people have and the meanings that they generate. Clearly, an assumption is made that the more reflective a person or group is upon the material circumstances of everyday life, the more likely they are to generate critical meanings that will seek to challenge normative orders.

This assumption is associated with the degree of autonomy that the human mind has from the social structures of everyday life. So, yes, human beings create and reproduce, value and legitimate social structures; celebrate and revile sets of social relations, *etc.* Social structures offer a range of spheres of influence for thinking and doing. Cultures are replete with symbolic aspects of these lived, active experiences. These social structures should also be 'extended' to acknowledge the question of resources and the natural and physical environment which clearly affect people's lives.

One of the key issues, therefore, is what agents or agencies make a difference to society and self. At this juncture we might well ask how professionals are more or less likely to evaluate their roles and their place in the social structures that act as the dynamic context of professional practice. Contemporary British sociology has not been without its reflectors upon these concerns.

Basil Bernstein's Durkheim-inspired structuralist theorising about the transformation of cultures has been one such contribution that is relevant here. Bernstein's writing consistently focuses on the conditions of change or non-change, and he is interested in the values that promote change or defend the status quo.

> "Bernstein argues that, in principle, contemporary state schools are in a process of change and transition - from social arrangements founded upon and manifest in, mechanical solidarity, to those associated with organic solidarity. Let us enumerate briefly those features of school organisation which Bernstein seeks to capture. Under the 'old' order, teacher and pupil roles are relatively fixed and determinate. Pupils, for example, are categorised, grouped and processed in terms of a few generic categories: age, sex and ability are major dimensions of such schemes. Units of social organisation are arranged in such a way as to maximise internal homogeneity, and the attributes used to classify pupils (and teachers) are regarded as fixed and stable. 'Ability', for example, will be treated as a more

or less stable attribute, used to classify pupils in the same way across years and across school subjects. Pupils would thus be allocated to forms or streams on the basis of such measured ability: there would be little mobility between streams, and pupils in a given stream or form would remain together for substantial amounts of their school work. Under such conditions, pupils are placed within the school on the basis of what pass for ascribed roles or characteristics.

As schools shift in organisation and ideology towards principles of organic solidarity, on the other hand, the emphasis moves towards the establishment of achieved roles for pupils. 'Ability', for instance, will no longer be thought of as a fixed and generic attribute. Rather, ability will be portrayed as a process, which is realised in the context of learning, and of interaction between teachers and taught. Hence, ability may be thought to be manifested differently in different pedagogic contexts: pupils maybe placed in sets for different school subjects, for instance. They are less likely to be placed in fixed structural units, which uniquely define the individual pupil's position within the school. Pupil's roles are, therefore, more flexible - or at any rate potentially so. School careers are achieved in terms of individual biographies, rather than ascribed in terms of pre-determined structural attributes or classes (in the most general sense of that term).

A parallel shift is suggested for teachers' roles in school. Under conditions of 'mechanical' solidarity, the social arrangements of the staff tend to follow disciplinary or subject lines. Subject departments tend to define the teacher's role: here again we find it is a matter of ascription and professional attributes, which are socially defined as relatively fixed. But the order changeth. The teacher's role, Bernstein suggests, is increasingly fragmented: classroom teaching of school subjects is supplemented by wider pastoral and careers duties. As the range of school subjects taught also becomes increasingly diverse, so the division of labour within the teaching staff becomes more complex, diffused and fragmented. Here too then, the person's role or biography is one which is to be made actively or accomplished rather than being given.

These shifts are paralleled by changes in pedagogy, curriculum and social control. The teacher ceases to operate solely as the provider of standard routines and solutions, and becomes the creator of problems for the pupils to solve. Pedagogy thus stresses pupil-discovery and self-discovery. The means of learning are valued, as much as or more than, its ends."

(Atkinson, 1985, p.25-26)

On the other side of the coin, Neil Keddie has considered an important social institution in the light of the individuation concerns.

In 'Adult Education: an ideology of individualism' (Keddie, 1980 in Thomson), Keddie argues that the claim for the 'uniqueness' of adult education as compared with the rest of education is an ideology that actually requires examination. Part of the current ideology of adult education is the student-centred, meeting the student-learner's needs issue. Another linked issue for Keddie is the increasing emphasis on professionalisation.

> "The ideology of adult education achieves, for practitioners, a promise to their clientele that their primary concern will be with students' needs and interests; and equally important, it operates to combat the marginality of adult education to the education system and helps to confirm practitioners' professional identities."

(Keddie, p.46)

Does the relatively low status of adult education threaten the professional identity or sense of self-worth of those practitioners engaged in it? What measures *within* the conventional ideology might such professionals use to combat this? It would seem that, for the practitioners, most adult education is an attempt to reach those who have experienced the least formal education or had least opportunities. If this is true, then this is somewhat ironic in placing this activity in a context of social differentiation and access to education. In this sense, it is really a class issue! However, this class analysis runs contrary to the belief held in adult education about *continuing* education. But what is it that is being continued? Adult education is a *person*-centred, rather than a subject-centred activity. I raise this matter here because so much of the education of professionals also claims the same pedigree. Individual need rather than achievement becomes the focus. However, adult education, like professional education, reproduces the value(s) of individualism as expressed through access to education. Does this then create, reinforce and reproduce the contradictions of individualistic values compared with: (a) service *for* and within the community/society; and (b) the emancipation of a class through *social*, as distinct from individual transformations?

As I have stated at the beginning of this section, the increased access to education and the professions has been seen as one of *the* fundamental examples of a more open and egalitarian society. But as we have seen, the critics of the professions are not convinced that has meant a better society or the liberation of our society from contradictions. Professionals continue to claim that they are altruistic and exist to give service to society rather than themselves. Most sociology is extremely sceptical of that claim and if we are on the threshold of a major reappraisal of the nature and role of the professional in our society, we must ask these questions. What is the bill of goods that society is to be sold in the era of the 'new professional'? One of my central concerns with the concept of the reflective practitioner is to ask precisely what qualitative differences in the nature, role and orientation of professional practitioners is anticipated as a consequence of a proposed rethinking of and refocusing on, practice?

Reflective Practice and the Reflective Practitioner

The concept of the 'reflective practitioner' has been developed in two areas of professional education. In the last ten years in America, Australia and Britain, people involved in teacher education, who have been concerned about the inadequacies of previous approaches and especially the lack of relationship between theory and practice, have discussed the idea of reflective practice as one approach to remedying these deficiencies (Zeichner 1984, Zeichner and Teitelbaum 1982, Goodman 1984, Zeichner 1986). Over the same period Schon's experiments in the education of a number of different professions led to an analysis of the epistemology of professional practice that opposes 'reflective' to the more common 'technocratic' model of practice (Argyris and Schon 1974, Schon 1983 and 1987). There are some signs of similar thinking emerging among nurse educators, but without reference to Schon's work or the development in education. I am also very interested in the highly relevant work of Stephen Brookfield on developing critical thinkers. The overlaps between the ideas and strategies of Brookfield, Schon, Zeichner and others is considerable and I shall want to elaborate on this aspect of the reflective practitioner debates later in this section of my essay (Brookfield 1987).

My aim in this section of the essay is to offer an account of the recent debates around the concepts of reflective practice and the reflective practitioner, especially in the context of what I have already said about professions and practice. However, whatever I say in this section of the essay will be seeing these debates in the 'practical' context of *professional education*. I want to argue through my view that it is only really relevant to discuss the concept of reflective practice if this is located alongside a discussion about developing and delivering a curriculum for change.

In the UK, Peter Jarvis has been arguing along similar lines, particularly in relation to debates around the nature of professional knowledge:

> "...at the foundation of every occupation claiming professional status is knowledge and its application."
>
> *(Jarvis, 1983, p.29)*

And it is to Jarvis that I would initially turn to locate my concerns about the interrelationship between professional education *in general*, knowledge and practice. Knowledge, Jarvis argues,

> "...may be seen as a level of awareness, consciousness or familiarity gained by experience, learning or thinking."
>
> *(Jarvis, op. cit. p.66)*

Jarvis, like many concerned with the education of professionals sees the need to discuss the concept of knowledge in relation to the curriculum devised and delivered. The relationship between the espoused aims of professional education or training, the nature of appropriate knowledge and its location in a programme of professional socialisation and social control, *is* problematic and requires explanation and exploration. The overwhelming convenionality here is misleading.

> "The aim of professional education is self-evident, to produce a competent pracitioner..."
>
> *(Jarvis, op. cit. p.48)*

But what does this really mean for all concerned?

> "... the process should produce recruits to the profession that have a professional ideology, especially in relation to understanding good practice and service. Secondly, that the educational process should provide the new recruit with sufficient knowledge and skills, or the continuing practitioners with enhanced knowledge and skills, to enter, or to continue in, the profession ... the process should result in the practitioner developing an increased sense of critical awareness."
>
> *(Jarvis op. cit. p.48)*

Jarvis is moving directly from the very conventional notions of why persons are educated for work in the professions to embrace the idea that this means that these persons are acquiring bodies of specified knowledge as part of their acculturation *and* that these knowledges should, but do not necessarily, already include a critical perspective on those knowledges.

This section of my essay is an attempt to develop an understanding of reflective practice and what it is to be a reflective practitioner. However, what is central to my entire project here is to locate this within a discussion about what passes for knowledge within and among the professions. Particularly I want to discuss the place of actual everyday professional practice in the processes that establish knowledges, understandings, ideas, *etc.*, about being professional and part of a profession.

> "However, the situation of practice may be designed, practice must be central to professional education rather than peripheral to it."
>
> *(Argyris and Schon, 1974)*

On the question of the centrality of practice issues, Argyris and Schon make it clear that self-consciously or reflectively or not, the professional does take action.

> "A profession then, not only has a practice, but also a theory of action in which that practice can become a reproducible, valid technique. This means that the job of professional education consists not only in teaching technique, but in teaching the methods by which behavioural worlds in which techniques work can be created."

(Argyris and Schon, 1974, p.149)

This is a key issue and brings me to an argumentative point about the character of the professions as a culture which is organised in such ways that are more or less likely to allow, permit or encourage changes to take place. Argyris, Schon and others cited above do emphasise the question of traditional structures of the professions that need to be changed. No one really doubts that a few professional practitioners here and there might change. It is also possible that specific groups may see themselves as change agents. This may be a major dimension of the professional educator's role to act as agents of change. Throughout the 'people-worker' professions, educational experiences in pre- and in-service contexts can and do facilitate the cultivation of *individuals* as change agents, but, does this make fundamental inroads into the structures?

It is quite clear that we have at least two major issues in view at the same time. Firstly, there is the whole debate about the nature of professions and whether or not certain members, or self-cultural groupings within any profession, are reflective practitioners, engage in reflective practice (or are working on it?) Does this really focus upon those members of a profession who are directly concerned with the education of the next generation of practitioners?

Secondly, if this last point is true to a greater or lesser extent, what educational strategies are being adopted and delivered in terms of the curriculum, *etc.,* that intend to produce professional practitioners who are, by definition, reflective practitioners? Those issues are going to be the real foci of my attention in this part of my essay and they will, quite intentionally, keep criss-crossing each other in my exposition. One current example might prove illuminating here. The Central Council for Education and Training in Social Work (CCETSW) has recently (1989) published its guidelines for the Diploma in Social Work. These guidelines have been used by curriculum designers to create an educational programme for social-work practitioners, with, for example, reference to 'The Core Skills of Social Work':

- COGNITIVE SKILLS
- INTERPERSONAL SKILLS
- DECISION-MAKING SKILLS
- ADMINISTRATIVE SKILLS
- SKILLS IN USING RESOURCES

In turn, these skills and their acquisition are related to 'Competence in Social Work Practice', which includes the aim that social workers should 'take responsibility for their professional practice', which, in turn, requires practitioners to 'reflect upon their work'.

Let me now map out the debate on the concepts of reflective practice and the reflective practitioner. I have already argued above for the relevant link between any professional embracing reflective practice *and* the role of the professional practitioner in educating the next generation. In this respect it is well worth starting with Zeichner and those other voices directly concerned with reflective teaching-teachers. If any professional practitioner is to take on the education of others they are, by definition, engaging in the life and times of 'another', *i.e.*, they are not only a nurse, or midwife or social worker or youth worker or sociologist, they are also a teacher:

> "Reflective teaching . . .occurs when you question and clarify why you have chosen your classroom methods, procedures and content. It also includes studying the school environment in relation to those choices to determine how the environment encourages or hinders reflective teaching. Reflective teaching is an on-going process that involves careful re-examination of what you have done and the social context in which it was done in order to help you do what you wanted to do better. It is thinking analytically about your goals, your teaching actions, and your teaching environment and using those thoughts to improve your future teaching."

> *(Zeichner, 1984)*

Although Zeichner is focusing his attention on 'teaching' in the schooling/education sense, I would argue that his observations could be equally well applied to other occupational groups that I would call 'people-workers'. These could be social workers, nurses or youth and community workers, for example, I say this in part because Zeichner is not just commenting on the *techniques* of the practice action, but rather on the contexts of any goal-orientated action. While some teachers, like any other practitioner, might carry out their tasks in a very unreflective way there is a need to move from this routine mode of human action to a more reflective one.

The work of John Dewey is interesting here. He suggested that there is high level of 'taken for grantedness' in the routine day-to-day action of many practitioners. Tasks are defined from 'outside' and the practitioner responds accordingly. In contrast, Dewey suggests that reflective action is "active, persistent and careful consideration of any belief or supposed form of knowledge in light of the grounds that support it and further consequences to which it leads." (Dewey, 1933, p.9)

Now, when you consider that this was written in the 1930s, it is chastening to consider the limits to progress made since then.

For Dewey there were three key characteristics of reflective action: open-mindedness, responsibility and whole-heartedness.

I would argue that a Dewey type model would be applicable to any current curriculum discussions for 'people-worker' practitioners. A great deal of the debates surrounding changes in social work or nursing practice say where a certain amount of this 'Dewey type' reorientation has already taken place is 'running ahead' of changes to the educational programmes that seek to prepare such practitioners.

I do not want to say much more about these issues here; they are taken up in the next section; but it is worth commenting on the contribution of Goodman (1984) and Zeichner and Teitelbaum (1982). Goodman focuses on the use of teaching practice as a means to an end, the end being the development of a reflective practitioner. She seeks to offer a contrast between rational and intuitive reflection; rational thought is characterised as:

> "...the organisation of information, selection of categories, dissection of the whole into parts, sequential thought progression, critical judgement of correctness, and

> explanatory language systems; intuitive
> thought involves imagination, humour, non-
> judgemental associations, emotions, inte-
> gration and synthesis, holistic perception,
> tacit sensitivity and understanding, and non-
> sequential thought expression."

(Goodman, 1984, p.19).

Her experience with the interrelation between teaching practice and student seminars to consider that practice, led to the belief that, for really reflective practice to take place, rational and intuitive thinking need integrating.

The Applied Education course at Oxford Polytechnic uses an ethnographic case study approach much like that advocated by Zeichner and Teitelbaum (1982). The student teachers are encouraged to take on the role of participant observer, which allows them to be engaged in practice, which may well be task-orientated, but which pushes them towards reflection upon this practice. This does raise questions for me about the way we might define the contexts and environment for 'learning about' practice.

In my experience of designing and delivering curricula for 'people-worker' practitioners I have become aware of pro-blems associated with the assumptions we may all make about developing reflective practice. Put bluntly, it may be a good deal easier to inspire our students to being reflective practitioners than it is to engage our colleagues or ourselves in these changes. One problem I have addressed throughout this essay is that of replacing one rather rigid orthodoxy with another in a very unthinking 'technical' way. I have experienced many examples of teachers-lecturers carefully addressing reflective issues and practices with their students, which are narrowly to do with an aspect of the 'professional practice' in question. However, these very same deliverers of the new curriculum are invariably unreflective in regard to the implications of the very environment of learning that they are engaged in. For the students, their education gets in the way of their education!

Kolb and Fry (1975) see the learning cycle as any experience which occurs within a complex integration of all three dimensions, *i.e.,* cognitive, affective and psychomotor, with possibly one of them being dominant. The experience may be facilitated by the teacher practitioner, although it may occur in the events of everyday living or working. Students may observe a situation, reflect upon it and learn, and the teacher practitioner may remain oblivious that a learning situation has occurred.

Hence, it may be seen that the human being does not merely receive a stimulus and respond to it - he or she has to think about it! Reflection is a significant element in human learning and one that it is important for the teacher practitioner to take into consideration in providing students with the opportunities to learn about aspects of the practical situation. However, reflection itself is not a simple process that occurs automatically or only at one level. Meilrow (1981) has suggested that there are *seven* levels of reflectivity:

Reflectivity - awareness of seeing, thinking or acting.
Affective reflectivity - awareness of feelings
Discriminant reflectivity - assessment of the efficiency of reflection in the context of reality
Judgemental reflectivity - being aware of the subjective value judgements about reflections
Conceptual reflectivity - assessment of whether the theoretical concepts employed are sufficient to explain perceived reality
Psychic reflectivity - considering the adequacy of the evidence employed to explain perceived reality
Theoretical reflectivity - awareness that taken-for-granted assumptions may be less than sufficient to explain perceived reality.

As one of the main aims of education, teacher practitioners should strive to produce critically aware fellow practitioners rather than recruits to the profession who merely conform to the theory and practice with which they are presented.

It may be seen that reflection not only occurs at the second stage in the learning cycle, but it also occurs in the third stage of formulating abstract concepts. Opportunity should be given by teacher practitioners for students to reflect upon their experiences and try to draw theoretical conclusions about them, conclusions about which the learner may still wish to be critical. Finally, the learner has to test the implications of the learning in new situations. Such a test may itself become a new experience that reactivates the whole process once again, or it may become new knowledge that the learner commits to memory, *etc.*

In precisely the same way, the experience may pose a problem for the student who may then endeavour to solve it through a process of reflection that leads to possible solutions which need testing, *etc.* Hence, both active learning and problem-solving may be viewed as similar processes which actually continue throughout the life-span. The process of reflection is, therefore, quite critical to learning and it is one that must influence the way that the teacher practitioner performs her role. For instance, he or she must:

1. Be prepared to let the learner think things out for themselves
2. Ask sufficient, relevant questions to encourage the process of reflection
3. Allow the learner to think things through at her or his own pace
4. Not seem too anxious that the learner should actually reach a conclusion

5.   Not expect that the learner will necessarily arrive at the same conclusion as she herself or himself has reached

6.   Not pressurise the student to reject solutions with which the Teacher Practitioner disagrees.

By this approach the teacher practitioner demonstrates recognition of the adulthood and maturity of the learner and encourages autonomy and independence, which are both essential attributes in the practice of nursing, midwifery and health visiting, as with most other 'people-work' professions.

I now want to focus my attention on the work of Schon, Argyris and their associates. A crucial source of ideas about reflective practice is Schon's work on the epistemology of practice (Schon, 1983). Schon argues that the kind of 'reflection-in-action' engaged in by competent professional practitioners has a kind of rigour both like and unlike the rigour of scholarly research and controlled experiment, but he is equally concerned with limits and implications.

It is worth considering Schon's own sketch of his motives for developing ideas on the reflective practitioner. In the preface to his 1987 text on *Educating the Reflective Practitioner,* he outlines his initial project as follows:

> "In the early stages of the journey, I planned a book on professional knowledge and education. Later it became clear to me that it would be necessary to split the book in two. In the first part, published in 1983 as *The Reflective Practitioner*, I argued for a new epistemology of practice, one that would stand the question of professional knowledge on its head by talking as its point of departure the competence and artistry already embedded in skilful practice -

especially, the reflection-in-action (the 'thinking what they are doing while they are doing it') that practitioners sometimes bring to situations of uncertainty, uniqueness and conflict. In contrast, I claimed, the professional schools of contemporary research unive-rsities give privileged status to systematic, preferably scientific, knowledge. Technical rationality, the schools' prevailing epistemology of practice, treats professional competence as the application of privileged knowledge to instrumental problems of practice. The schools' normative curriculum and separation of research from practice leave no room for reflection-in-action, and thereby create - for educators, practitioners, and students - a dilemma of rigor or relevance. The argument of *The Reflective Practitioner* implies a question: What kind of professional education would be appropriate to an epistemology of practice based on reflection-in-action? I left the question unanswered there, to be answered here."

(Schon, 1987, pp. xi/xii)

Later in my essay I shall return to Schon's question myself and ask some questions of my own about professional education and the development of the curriculum.

For now, though, let me return to the development of what might be called Schon's epistemology of practice.

In my section on 'The professions...' I emphasised the growing disenchantment with professions and professionals. Schon's work is very much concerned with the realisation within professional ranks that all is not well. The complexity of the social and other problems facing them, the reduction in legitimation given to professionals linked with an increasingly influential 'alternative agenda' challenging the professions' right to claim expertise has created a crisis in confidence. This work of Schon's develops the work of the 1970s conducted jointly with Argyris (1974).

Schon, alone, and with Argyris, has argued that a body of theory does underpin and inform the day-to-day action of the professional practitioner. These practitioners are theo-rists, their action, their practice draws on this developed work culture. Essentially, these theories are what Schon calls 'theories in use' and are a combination of three kinds of ideas about effective work practices. These ideas are about what approaches work well in particular contexts, some explanations as to why they work well, and thirdly a readiness to alter ways of working as dictated by a recognisable change in circumstances.

Brookfield characterises this as follows:

> "These theories are developed in certain recognisable stages. Educators or helping professionals, for example, observe their actions and those of their colleagues to see what approaches work well with the learners and clients with whom they are concerned. They develop hunches about how they might alter their practice and test these out in different contexts.
>
> They become critically reflective conc-erning what approaches work best, in which situations and why these are successful.
>
> In many professionals' work activities, creativity, playing hunches, intuition and informed guesswork are central of what is considered appropriate practice."

> (*Brookfield, 1987, p.152*)

From this argument we can see that for Schon, *et al*, what professional practitioners actually do may not in fact be drawn from textbooks. Their practice tends to be developed from the meanings they place upon their experiences as practitioners and the relation of this reflection upon their goals as action takers. These 'theories in use' are just like cognitive maps. This is in the contextual realm of my discussion of these ideas. I would call this dimension the conditions of practice, because we are clearly talking about both the content of practice and its form.

'Theories in use' are contrasted with so-called 'espoused theories' which are part and parcel of the agreed, normative knowledge order of the professional in question. What we conventionally see is that any profession espouses what theories should and do underpin its practice. This is usually legitimated in suitable ways, for example, via well-established curricula for a profession's education courses. These may, in fact, be part of what would usually be called role expectations, consistently, through socialisation and social control mechanisms, reinforcing appropriate thoughts and deeds. However, this may well be an example of widespread role conflicts for practitioners.

> "Theories in use are kept private, since they frequently contradict many of the appa-rently revered tenets of espoused theories. Even when espoused theories do not work, there may be a reluctance on the part of many professionals to make public their critical analysis, since to do is to appear to be either incompetent (unable to apply theories correctly to specific situations) or heretical."

> *(Brookfield, 1987, p.153)*

These pages could certainly be filled with arguments supporting the view that the ideas and practices of many workers, individually or collectively, come into conflict with the goals and expectations of their employing organisations. What Schon and others are emphasising is that practitioners do reflect upon their roles (and their training/socialisation into them) and find prevailing orthodoxies unsatisfactory. This does, of course, include their personal role performance. My own experience of teaching the 'pre-service' social worker would confirm that considerable doubts about the expectations associated with the work roles open to them in training and beyond are problematic. Again it is worth recapping on my earlier comments that one of the important contexts for increasing numbers of practitioners is that they work within an organisational framework that is more or less determining.

If, as a consequence of developing 'theories in use', the practitioner comes to see that this practice actually bears fruit of the kind he or she savours, then the practitioner will also have to devise strategies to deal with conflicts. The following comment by Pollard and Tann serves as a good indicator of a general problem.

> "... in the post-War years, and up to the early 1970s, there was a significant degree of consensus about the aims of state education - a prevailing ideology. In an era of economic expansion, prominent goals included striving towards equality of opportunity and making the best use of the nation's resource of young people. In primary education, the Plowden report...provided official support for child-centred teaching methods and this legitimated the particular way of teaching, which became known as 'progressivism'. The focus was on the 'growth' of individual

children, on their all-round development and on the quality of classroom relationships.

However, in the early- to mid-1970s, with economic recession gradually deepening and confidence decreasing, the progressive ideology was challenged. Indeed, it was seen by some to represent an ideology of 'trendy teachers and educationalists'. . .

Thus, the dominant patterns of thinking about primary school practice have changed considerably in recent years. Teachers are often required to respond to such development as new priorities supplant old ones. Awareness of the concept of ideology makes it more likely that the values of interests that may be behind new proposals will be considered by reflective teachers."

(Pollard and Tan, 1987)

My own experience of teaching sociology and social policy to social workers and post-registration nurses in recent years would confirm that the concept of ideology, if well developed through clear examples of the contexts of policy and practice, provides these practitioners with an invaluable analytical tool. This is especially important in regard to conventional bodies of knowledge and received ideas. As Schon reflects:

"Complexity, instability and uncertainty are not removed or resolved by applying specialised knowledge to well-defined tasks. If anything, the effective use of specialised knowledge depends on a prior restructuring of situations that are complex and uncertain. An artful practice of the unique case appears

> anomalous when professional competence is
> modelled in terms of application of esta-
> blished techniques to recurrent events.
> Problem setting has no place in a body of
> professional knowledge concerned exclu-
> sively with problem solving. The task of
> choosing among competing paradigms of
> practice is not amenable to professional
> expertise."
>
> *(Schon, 1983, p.19)*

One aspect of Schon's work that I find relevant to my own experience is his concern to identify what it is that practitioners actually do as they go about their day-to-day routine.

Dowie and Elstein refer to Schon's work in their recent contribution to the debate on professional judgement (Dowie and Elstein, 1988). They concentrate on the medical pro-fession to make clearer the basis of clinical judgement and decision-making. What pressures are there, internally and externally, to the profession that have come to effect practices? Has there been a legitimation crisis; have difficult questions about accountability been more frequently posed? Dowie and Elstein ask how much of the development of explanatory systems has been incorporated into a profession or professional education?

For example, are professional educators up-to-date with thinking, perhaps from diverse sources, which may be relevant to their practice?

> "On the contrary, Schon sees clinical wisdom
> and expertise residing precisely in the ability
> to accomplish the tremendously difficult
> synthesizing task...without resort to formal
> analysis. Expert clinicians move efficiently to
> the appropriate resolution of problems

> where 'resolution' encompasses the 'fram-
> ing' or 'setting' of the problem as well as its
> 'solving' once it has been framed."

(Dowie and Elstein, 1988, p.3)

Not the least of my concerns here is the value we do or might attach to this 'artistic' or 'intuitive' skill, clearly associated with experience of problem resolution (or not) and the practitioner's reflection upon the whole process. If this is the reality, how can this be learnt by newcomers to a profession? Only through their experience of practice? What can they learn to prepare them for these situations? In addition to these questions, Schon identifies major problems for the professional because of the dominance of what he calls technical rationality; "instrumental problem solving made rigorous by the application of scientific theory and technique." Schon clearly believes that there is a hierarchy of knowledge in professions and the preparation for prof-essional practice, that puts an unambiguous science orien-tation to solving problems above that of learning and theorizing through practice. For Schon, this 'positivist epistemology' has come to be dominant throughout its institutionalisation in the last two hundred years, or over about the same time as the prodigious growth of the professions in our societies.

Very largely, because of the traditional status accorded to the professions, other occupational groups have sought to emulate them in recent years. Moving away from the routine action associated with many so-called 'lower professions' like social work, youth and community work and nursing, has resulted in a movement towards technical rationality. This movement has taken part largely because of the ideological struggles around what constitutes an/the appropriate knowledge base for the aspiring profession in question. Ironically, then, in the quest for status-seeking, focus on 'scientificness' may well steer practitioners away from the artistic and intuitive. The desire to fix the quality of professional education to a set of competences is likely to upgrade the much more rigid and standardised 'technicist' and 'scientificness' approaches.

If, as many observers suspect, an increasing number of 'people-worker' occupational groups seeking a higher status decide to go down the scientific road, concerns with positivistic theory rather than with practice are going to dominate curriculum design. The up-and-coming professions have looked at the more traditional professions and invariably equated power with bodies of scientifically informed knowledge. However, as I have suggested above, most practitioners, in even the well-established professions, do not necessarily actually behave in this way.

Schon is particularly concerned with an aspect of practice that is most open to ambiguity, where the practitioner is most vulnerable:

> "...indeterminate zones of practice - uncertainty, uniqueness, and value conflict - escape the canons of technical rationality. When a problematic situation is uncertain, technical problem solving depends on the prior construction of a well-formed problem - which is not in itself a technical task. When a practitioner recognises a situation as unique, she cannot handle it solely by applying theories or techniques derived from her store of professional knowledge. And in situations of value conflict, there are no clear and self-consistent ends to guide the technical selection of means.
>
> It is just these indeterminate zones of practice, however, that practitioners and critical observers of the professions have

come to see with increasing clarity over the past two decades as central to professional practice. And the growing awareness of them has figured prominently in recent controversies about the performance of the professions and their proper place in society."

(Schon, 1987, pp.6-7)

When Schon comes to think about the way in which professional practitioners deal with the out-of-the-ordinary in their everyday working lives, he argues that they deal with it in essentially the same way as we all do in everyday life. We take another look, with reflect, we consider a reframing.

The essential leap forward for Schon is into reflection-in-action; the practitioner:

> "...becomes a researcher in the practice context. He is not dependent on the categories of established theory the unique case. His inquiry is not limited to a deliberation about means, which depends on a prior agreement about ends. He does not keep means and ends separate, but defines them interactively as he frames a problematic situation. He does not separate thinking from doing, ratiocinating his way to a decision, which he must later convert to action. Because his experimenting is a kind of action, implementation is built into his inquiry. This reflection-in-action can proceed, even in situations of uncertainty or uniqueness, because it is not bound by the dichotomies of Technical Rationality."

(Schon, 1983, p.68)

It seems to me that Schon is essentially concerned with communicative processes. 'Reflection-in-action' as a process "involves a reflective conversation with the situation." This concern with communication is, therefore, both internal to and external to the practitioner. I would argue that this view is close to what many sociologists refer to as 'interaction order'. When faced with a problem, particularly one to do with bringing about effective communication between practitioner and client, the former must take into account the 'frame' of action. These 'frames' will be imposed through all manner of agency including the expectations of management seeking task orientation perhaps, and the expectations of clients. The practitioner must 'listen'; this is essentially research, which, over time, builds up into a repertoire that is 'artistic' in its character.

In his analysis of forms of knowledge as related to practice, Schon is consistently moving the debate towards an embracing of a self-conscious reflective practice. Most of what he has to say about the 'present' state of professional practices focuses and refocuses attention upon the need to change.

> "There seems then, to be some growing recognition of the need for co-operative inquiry within adversarial contexts. The ideas of reflective practice leads to a vision of professions as agents of society's reflective conversation with its situation, agents who engage in co-operative inquiry within a framework of institutionalised contention. The question remains, however, whether it is utopian, in the pejorative sense, to suppose that professions who occupy key roles in the public policy process can learn on a broad

basis to engage in reciprocal reflection-in-action."

(Schon, 1983, p.353)

An important aspect of this 'utopia' of which Schon speaks is that, as he acknowledges, not all that many professionals are self-conscious reflective practitioners. The idea that professionals can/will be reflective practitioners operating within a changing and changed social structure and/or occupational culture is an abstract idea constantly counterposed to the social reality of how most professionals and their cultures are now.

In this context I would want to cite the work of Zygmunt Bauman, who argues that culture does fundamentally represent the antidote to alienation. Culture is that way in which human beings collectively aspire to deal with the contradictions of living and prospering in their time and space contexts. Occupational cultures are clearly examples of this. The professions, as I have argued already in this essay, have created countless symbolic aspects to their culture boundary maintenance. In the main, this is in order to preserve what they have come to believe is true and proper. In this situation, the affinity and the opposition between reflective practice and radical practice praxis become clearer. Both envision a universe, which, while originating in the given social relationships, also liberates individuals from these relationships. The freedom of all secures the freedom of each!

What I have already said about espoused theories, resonates with Schon's comments on technical rationality and the reification of practice ideas that drive the practitioner away from putting human matters back into arguments about practice relationships of all kinds. All reification is forgetting. What I have already said about knowledge and human interests and communicative action is relevant here.

In drawing this section of my essay to a conclusion, I would reiterate my belief that many 'people-worker' occupational groups, whether established professions, or ones seeking to be seen as such, are faced with real problems. These problems have been outlined in my Introduction, where I emphasised the value orientations of certain professions in relation to the key debates around human needs. The problems confronting the professions in general and individual members of those occupational cultures were taken up and developed in my section on 'The Professions'. What I have attempted to do in this section of the essay is relate some of these problems the professions have to the organisation of forward-looking educational practices. I have drawn on Schon, and other commentators, precisely because they have also moved from a general assessment of the state of professional practice to debating questions about the education and/or training of future generations of practitioners. It is quite clear (and my own working experience with social workers and nurses bears this out) that an increasing number of professions, and more particularly those within a profession charged with the responsibility of preparing the next generation of practitioners, are looking to higher education to help resolve their problems. However, higher education tends to be rather elitist, concerned with abstract theory and the production of bodies of knowledge that are essentially part of a discrete discourse among the academics themselves, rather than in the 'real' world of 'people-working' practice. There is already considerable antipathy between certain members of professions over the issue of who 'owns' the practice. In the short term at least, I can see these difficulties increasing. Schon and most of the others discussed above do have the advantage of standing outside particular professions while offering comment on and analysis of recent trends. However, by putting questions about the centrality of practice on the agenda of curriculum debates they have made a valuable contribution on both sides of the Atlantic.

I would not want to sound too pessimistic about the future, or to suggest that only dissent and disagreement lie ahead in the discussion about appropriate curricula for the professions. This is far from the case: these problems are being systematically addressed by the professions and, in particular, by the educators of practioners. They have been discussing the crucial importance of developing a curriculum for professional practice education that incorporates some element of reflective practice (for example, Clarke, 1986).

It is, however, an area of curriculum design, delivery and evaluation that is beset with some real difficulties. The problems with an over positivistic or scientific knowledge base, the elitist nature of higher education, the wariness and reluctance to address new agendas of many practitioners 'in the field' and the sheer methodological difficulties of actually putting some very good ideas about the education of professional practitioners into practice. How can what might seem very laudable ideas about *preparing* reflective practitioners be translated into a curriculum that will make this happen while remaining open and critical about the whole educational process? It is these issues that I shall turn to in the next section.

Turning the Concept of Reflective Practice into Curriculum Reality

At this point, I want to turn my attention of the social environment in which the 'New Professional', the emergent reflective practitioner, is to learn his or her craft.

It is in this environment that the education of the new generation of professionals will be located. These teachers may be 'housed' in different places, of course, and their primary practice, day-to-day occupational activity may vary considerably. For example, we might discuss the teacher based in the educational institution primarily responsible for putting on and running the course attended by the student. These teachers may regard themselves, and be regarded as, academics. They may be teacher or tutors who have a background in the professional practice that the course is concerned with. However, these teachers may well be located 'in the field' in one place or way or another and maintain some tenuous link with the educational institution. There are problems here that I want to discuss.

One important dimension of my discussion must be the generalised educational setting, or 'reflective practicum' as Schon calls it. It is in this environment Schon argues that students mainly learn by doing, with the help of coaching:

> "Their practicum is 'reflective' in two senses; it is intended to help students become proficient in a kind of reflection-in-action; and when it works well, it involved a dialogue of coach and student that takes the form of reciprocal reflection-in-action."

> *(Schon op. cit. Preface)*

I want to return to 'the practicum' idea later. Initially, though, I must address the question of who should teach the students, and illustrate this discussion by some extended reference to my own reflective practice as a teacher.

WHO SHOULD TEACH 'THE NEW PROFESSIONALS'?

One of the characteristics of a large number of Professional Education courses is that they borrow very heavily from other Professions' bodies of specialist knowledge - social science, science, *etc.* Indeed the regulatory bodies for most Professional Education insist upon courses including such interventions into the Curriculum. Part of the contradiction, that I wish to dwell upon, for these emergent occupational groups, is that they argue for the need to include such professional knowledge in their course of professional socialisation.

It seems to me that the gradual 'upgrading' of Professional education in most people's eyes - certificate to diploma to degree, *etc.*; one year to two to three years, *etc.* - is seen as a positive step towards achieving full professional status. However, this raises unresolved questions about the relative status of knowledge that make up the curriculum, as well as the relative status of theory and practice. What are the contexts and motivations here? Is the aim to introduce the student to some things that are new: skills, tasks, ideas, *etc.* In this situation what is the relationship between this 'new' knowledge/practice and what is already known/done? Secondly, when might we assume these new things become the student practitioners' *own*? Are they ever their *own*? Who do they have/need to share this knowledge and practice with? Even if we take these adoption/adaptation processes as problematic we also need to discuss in what ways/or what time do these things become less part of the teacher and more part of the student practitioner?

If, on the other hand, we are discussing advancing or developing the knowledge and skills of existing practitioners what are we taking as given and what is it that we are adding to or improving or developing? Are we asking a series of questions like:

1. How do you practice now?
2. What theories of practice is this based upon?
3. How and why do you want to improve upon and develop your practice? What do you feel you need to know, learn, *etc.* to make you a more effective, competent practitioner?

This raises questions about the imposition of a body of culturally (professionally) sanctified knowledge and practice. Is this what happens most of the time in the delivery of a pre-determined curriculum that is delivered to students regardless of their existing status, knowledge, experience, *etc*? How different might our orientation to practice (and teaching) be if we started from the premise that people of all statuses in these Professional Education situations already know and do a great deal. They may have quite well developed ideas 'of their own' (or as a self-conscious group) about what they want to do and how they feel is the best way to do it.

> "There are many practical implications here, for example, the negotiated curriculum, individual learning contracts, learning styles and choice of teaching methods.
>
> In the first of these examples, the negotiated curriculum, teachers and learners are not only engaged in discussing what is relevant, necessary, *etc.* to meet their range of needs, they are also almost certain to have to address the question of assessment and evaluation. My own experience of professionals in both pre- and in-service educational situations would certainly emphasise the inter- and intra-professional group variety. It seems to me that a good part of

> the discussions are contextualised by the training and education background of the 'students' in question. For example, almost without exception, I have found courses in post registration in-service programmes to be greatly influenced by their expectation that little or no negotiation is likely or possible in relation to the devising of the curriculum, its modes of delivery assessment, evaluation, *etc.*
>
> One feature of the debate on learning and/or cognitive styles has been the attempt to emphasise the argument that most teachers have little or no knowledge about the theory of these styles."
>
> *(Cross, 1976)*

This clearly has ramifications for discussions around reflective practice. In a formalised professional education context it would be essential for the educator to take into consideration the debates on learning and cognitive styles. The reflective practitioner would give due consideration to the ways in which interaction between teachers and learners takes place, particularly in terms of any on-going evaluation of the effectiveness of education programmes. The following perspectives on this debate merely give a flavour of the views on preferred styles of learning or teaching.

Ausubel (1978) talks of assimilation theory where meaning is derived from interaction, assimilation and incorporation of new and old material (*e.g.* using experiences as a starting point).

Bruner (1969) advocates discovery learning where meaning is derived from understanding and relating.

Students may use coding systems to classify or group information.

Gagne (1977) stresses the importance of the individual as a processor of information in which central components are cognitive not physical (Bruner, 1969, Gagne, 1977, Ausubel, 1978).

I would like to return to the question of experiential learning in due course by looking in particular at the ideas of David Kolb.

In order to consider some of these questions, I would like to focus attention initially on the role of the academic specialists, those who are not members of the Profession in question (*e.g.*, not nurses). Secondly, I will turn to the Professional practitioners themselves. So how can these emergent professions achieve their aims? Should they keep the specialist academic bodies of knowledge in their courses, separately marked out in the curriculum, but taught by the host practitioners themselves, *i.e.*, nurses, midwives or social workers who teach psychology or biology? (This is certainly relevant when an increasing number of nurses and other professional practitioners acquire degrees in academic disciplines.)

Or should they get psychologists or biologists to teach (have real control over) these specialist bodies of knowledge? Even when these problems are resolved, how are these bodies of specialist knowledge to be taught? What is assumed that needs to be learnt and how is it to be learnt? Are we looking at possible conflicts between pedagogy and andragogy?

The debate around the ideas of Malcolm Knowles is particularly relevant here.

Knowles developed the concept of andragogy in the context of the existing, so called, 'Romantic' curriculum innovations of the 1960s. This is characterised by its child/student centredness. It is cooperative rather than competitive; style and diversity are emphasised.

Andragogy in turn emphasises independence, self-direction, the existing experience of the student/learner, a problem-solving outlook, students learning what they need to know and learning organised around application.

Knowles argues that people are performance centred in their learning.

> "Knowles argues that andragogy is 'based on four assumptions about the characteristics of adult learners'. These are:
>
> (i) as a person matures, his self-concept moves from one of being a dependent personality toward one of being a self-directing human being;
> (ii) he accumulates a growing reservoir of experience that becomes an increasing resource for learning;
> (iii) his readiness to learn becomes oriented increasingly to the developmental tasks of his social roles;
> (iv) his time perspective changes from one postponed application of knowledge to immediacy of application, and accordingly his orientation toward learning shifts from one of subject-centredness to one of problem-centredness."
>
> *(Humphries, 1989, p.6)*

Knowles believes that adults increasingly devise their own goals for learning based on self-diagnosis of their needs and skills. The self-concept is an important aspect of this for Knowles as growing up takes the person from being reactive and dependent to pro-active and independent. These tendencies need to be harnessed for educational purposes. Given time I would have liked to look deeper at Knowles' arguments and the arguments of Shotter and social accountability (Shotter, 1984), but I can only refer the interested reader to the relevant literature (Knowles, 1973 and 1983). However, there are critics of Knowles. Jarvis, for example, argues that the time was right for Knowles to 'launch' his concept. Critics, like Day and Baskett, have argued that andragogy is not a theory of adult learning (a 'psychological' theory as such) but is an educational ideology rooted in an enquiry based learning and teaching paradigm. Critics would argue that insufficient research has been developed or evaluated to date to substantiate or deny the 'theory'. (Jarvis, 1984).

Several writers have commented on the obsessively individualistic nature of Knowles' arguments. Keddie argues that 'adult education' as practised and delivered in the UK is, by definition, based on an ideology of person-centredness. Ideal though this may seem from the point of view of the teacher and the student, she feels that it reproduces contradictions inherent in society that set the individual's interests against those of the community. (Keddie, 1980).

Law and Rubenson raise similar problems, arguing that most educational theory that focuses on the individual does not deal adequately with questions of the need for a theory of social transformation. Knowles' focus on the psychological as distinct from the social dynamics of change is seen as inadequate. (Law and Rubenson, 1988).

Those professions that have resisted inroads by non-practitioners, with their own specialist knowledges (particularly the social scientists in relation to health care?) are seen as out of date! One of the explanations for this view, as well as one of the contradictions in all this for Nursing,*etc.*, is that there has been a major shift towards a 'social' model of health care which seems to be, by definition, inviting a social scientific perspective. This, in turn, has had a significant bearing on the development of Professional Education in general and from my own perspective on these matters, it would seem that most critical comment on Professional Education has come from the 'Social' Sciences.

I would include here the work of many Educationalists contributing to both Adult and continuing education and Professional Education and training. I am certainly aware of arguments that emphasise the value to continuing self-development within a profession of knowledge related to experience and practice. It is also argued that for initiates to a 'caring or welfare' orientated profession there must be an acknowledgement of the 'adult' skills, understandings and insights, *etc.* that such people bring with them. (Jarvis, 1983).

Indeed, an increasing amount of literature in this field refers to the fundamental criteria for Professional Knowledge and seeks to emphasise that this knowledge is essentially a selection from knowledges in general that are considered by members of a Profession to be the foundation of their practice.

Comment continues to be made on the social and sub-cultural contexts of professional knowledge and the following list of criteria is fairly typical in stating what Professional Knowledge is:

1. Abstact and organised into a codified body of principles
2. Applicable, or thought to be applicable, to the concrete problems of living
3. Thought by the relevant members of society to be able to solve problems
4. That the possession of this knowledge means that problems can be solved
5. Should be created, organised, and transmitted by the profession
6. The profession should be arbiter over disputes about the validity of technical solutions, and
7. The amount of knowledge and difficulty of its acquisition should be great enough to give the

possessor an aura of mystery not given to ordinary people.

(Goode, 1973)

However, I do feel that a tendency among (even) social scientists is to be naively unaware of the implications of their power or influence in these matters of the Curriculum. Or is it that they are only too well aware of their ideological roles and seek to use and reproduce their position to enhance their own status?

So what role are non-professional practitioners, *i.e.* non-nurses, *etc.* going to play in all this? Are they going to continue to push for their involvement in courses of Professional Education? Why and with what justification? What are their motives for wanting the inclusion of their academic specialisms into the curriculum for courses of Professional Education? Or, indeed, what is their justification for the inclusion of themselves, these scientists and social scientists, *etc.* as arbiters or/and teachers of these specialised bodies of knowledge? Have they thought much about it?

There is a further complication here in that most of these scientists and social scientists, *etc.,* are employed as teachers or lecturers. What is their institutionally or self-assigned role or orientation? Are they seen as, do they see themselves as, scientists or social scientists, or teachers? This may make an important difference in relation to their professional culture, value-orientation. For example, do they devote more time and effort to developing their specialist knowledge as a biologist or sociologist or philosopher, or do they spend more time developing their professional practice as a teacher?

Now of course they might do both, but where do they turn for professional reference, role models, directional guidance, *etc.* What role strains or conflicts does this possible dichotomisation create? It is true that there are going to be some significant variations or value orientations here and actual differences in preparation for these roles? For example, how many lecturers in advanced FE/HE are actually 'trained' teachers? Are we likely to find a difference between their attitudes and practices towards and within courses of Professional Education, and that which we would find amongst trained teachers in the schooling system or non-advanced FE and its equivalents?

Indeed, sociologically speaking, more research, both nationally and locally, needs to be done to discover what these ranges of practitioners actually think and do. Recent studies of the Medical Profession suggest that doctors are great synthesizers of conventionally legitimated knowledge and practice and that little or no recourse is made to systematic analysis in the pursuit of problem-solving (Dowie and Elstein, 1988). How much reflection-in-action, on the practice process, does the Professional engage? These kind of questions need asking.

Most academics who make a considered decision to teach on Professional Education courses are dedicated to the task and develop a considerable understanding of the particular professional practice. This invariably includes considerable concern for the relevance and applicability of their specialist (academic) knowledge to the Profession in question. This is certainly my own experience. I have always wanted to know more about these contexts in relation to my educational strategies. However, they do remain as non-practitioners, on the outside. This is interesting, because most scientists and social scientists would join the chorus of academic voices that argue that theory without practice is sterile and eventually becomes reified. It is also, unfortunately, in my opinion, the case that in the era of 'marketing' and 'The Enterprise Culture' that many academic specialists jump on to the training 'bandwagon' as a means of survival. Such a motivation for action is not likely to lead to the most reflective practice or the more sensitive and empathetic orientations to the needs of Professional Education.

So what is it about their own practice as knowledge specialists that makes the academic specialist valuable? Is it in fact the relation between their own specialist/academic knowledge base and their practice as a teacher? Is it their experience and reflective practice as a teacher as much as anything else about them that makes them valuable to courses of Professional Education and adds credibility to their participation in Professional Education. (This credibility 'rule' or qualification may be very different from the conventional sources of legitimation of academics' participation, which I discuss elsewhere in this paper.)

In these circumstances, an experienced teacher-applicator of a science or social science with a highly sensitised orientation to the practice of other professions, educational needs, *etc.*, might actually be justifiably a member of a Professional Education 'team'. Other issues, therefore, enter into the arena for consideration, for example, commitment to a team of Professional Educators in relation to the curriculum, its design, development, delivery and evaluation. It may also embrace the question of research orientations and engagement in related aspects of Professional Education, *e.g.*, involvement in Fieldwork Teachers' courses. The Academic Specialist may also reasonably seek to legitimate her/his actions through the role of client focused/centred critic of Professional practice. The Academic specialist, because of her/his immersion in the knowledge base and up-to-dateness may believe that they, as good citizens, should keep the Professional Practitioners 'on their toes', or 'off the toes' of the clients?

My experiences and observations have convinced me that a substantial amount of specialist academic involvement in courses of Professional Education does little more than deliver, in a very segmented way, bodies of knowledge that are assumed to be appropriate to practice and its context. I have seen very little reflective practice that takes the professionals involved into the realms of applying their knowledge to a consideration of the course itself, to the learning and teaching on the course itself. Students of all kinds on courses of Professional Education are not encouraged to include the Professional Educational processes in question as part of their orientation to their practice.

This is not to deny the actual or possible relevance or usefulness of the specialist knowledge itself, but ironically these knowledges are usually delivered in a way and within a context of intention and motive that circumnavigate vital questions about the process of professional socialisation and social control that is happening. The most obvious, relevant example is the very question of the educational programme itself, which is invariably left underdeveloped as an issue for discussion. The agency of the specialist knowledge-monger is on the one-hand celebrated in the conventional manner, as a reservoir, and transmitter of, bodies of knowledge. This again is then denied, because the interactions that are taking place in order to devise and deliver the curriculum are not highlighted as critical. Now, one would hope that sociology can contribute a great deal here - in challenging assumptions, conventional wisdoms, *etc.* But this does mean taking some risks. The specialist can easily become a self-parody, caught contradictorily between enlightenment and obscurantism.

What is in it for the professional practitioners? Are they merely acknowledging the fact that most, if not all, of the statutory and regulatory bodies like ENB or CCETSW, *etc.* insist upon conventional sets of academic knowledges in the Professional Education curriculum? Do the practitioners really believe that they do not already know enough about the physical or the social or the psychological, *etc.*, in relation to the practice of their profession that they cannot teach it all themselves? To what extent has staff development in relation to professional practice and teaching on courses of Professional Education actually focused on these issues? One of the real, *i.e.*, already commonplace, problems here is that Professional Practitioners who run courses tend to marginalise the 'academics', while many of the 'academics' are accomplices in this process whereby the servicing phenomenon continues. Even members of the same academic department, but of differing professions, can stand by the customs and practices where consultation and teamwork are minimised. One group 'agrees' not to 'interfere' with the 'rights' or 'territory' of another group. Do the students benefit? What does this tell us about these various social actors? What does it tell us about the conditions, conventional wisdoms and expectations of their practice? One thing that seems clear to me is that these questions are not on the agenda in Professional Education. My suspicion is that even when they do get on to 'the agenda' the focus is the individual in a liberal-rationalist context that takes little or no notice of social dynamics.

How does all this relate to the development of lecturers in professional practice and lecturer practitioners in particular? If a professional practitioner becomes a whole time teacher-lecturer of professional practice does she/he become assimilated into a different set of values from those of the practitioner of that profession in general? How do they view the profession and its practice and how are they viewed in turn? Might we assume that those professional practitioners who take on a teaching role are more concerned with changing the profession in question? Again, what is their relationship with the bodies of specialist knowledge of that professional group? Are they 'merely' vehicles for the transmission of these legitimated bodies of knowledge? Are they only concerned with the inculcation of that knowledge into initiates as part of a process of professional socialisation and social control? And/or do these professionals see themselves directly concerned with questions about what it is that the professional practitioner needs to know/learn/practice? If so, are they going to spend more of their time on reflecting upon and generating theory about the profession which, despite their interest in and commitment to, they remain an outsider? I take it as read that we need to know more about these relationships and orientations. We need more facts about what people do with their time and how they perform their roles. We need to engage in the interpretive understanding of the subjective meanings of the various professionals concerned. If we pursue these questions, they do, in my opinion, heighten the contradictions of a practice-based, client centred and reflective approach when compared with the overwhelmingly characteristic 'scientific', technical-rationalistic approach. The latter has, and does, in my opinion, encourage an elitist posture by the professionals in question, seeing knowledge that is 'theory in abstract' based upon narrowly conceived and legitimated methodologies.

John Holmes, in his study of Youth and Community Work, sums this up well:

> "The logic of pursuing professionalism in the alternative model would be to emphasise the central importance of affective knowledge based on interpersonal understanding, and not to suffer from an inferiority complex regarding the apparent 'thinness' of a cognitive knowledge base. It would be to build on the diversified local structures as a first priority with a loose federation of local groups rather than try to establish a tight structure limited to professionals. It would clearly not lead to the establishment of salary scales in which the highest point for unqualified workers is automatically less than the lowest point for qualified workers. It would recognise that a career may well be

limited rather than see the development of a
career structure as an essential corollary of
professionalism."

(Holmes, 1981)

Let me now turn, as promised, to focus on some reflections
upon my practice as a teacher. At least initially I want to cast
these reflections in the context of the reality of preparing an
educational programme to educate for professional practice.

How do people become reflective professional practitioners? How can they 'learn' these 'skills' and how can we
'teach' them? Or what Schon (1987) calls 'teaching artistry
through reflection-in-action'.

When I set about preparing and delivering a curriculum
derived from sociology, I set out to reproduce myself a set of
truths I hold dear about the value of sociology and its
functions in our everyday lives.

At no time do I believe that there is a fixed volume or
amount of sociological knowledge that I must incorporate
into a curriculum and must deliver, assess students'
learning, *etc.* What I do expect is that I will first and foremost
assess, make judgements about the role and relevance of
sociology and sociological analysis for this person or group
etc., I ask myself (and other professional practitioners if
appropriate) what they would expect the learner to
accomplish or *know* at the end of this educational experience
or programme. This will affect how I visualise the curriculum
- what the component parts are for the overall design. I can
then consider what foundations or framework or structure I
want for the material I want to include. What do I consider is
essential for the learner to do, to understand, (and use
themselves - experience that understanding) before they can
move onto the next, more sophisticated stage. These later
stages may well be much more directed to the practical
applications of sociology for their own use. I do not want
students to keep referring to me, or even their books, to

know what to do in a situation, whether this be of a theoretical or practical, sociologically analytical situation. I intend an outcome of their learning to be their own self-confidence in the analytical skills they have acquired based, as they are, on sound theoretical foundations and applicatory judgement. Intuitive action for and towards analysis is what I move towards; what Schon calls 'knowing-in-action'.

I certainly do consider what any learner needs to know at the beginning of their educational programme that will enable them to learn more. The knowing in my sense is therefore not just bodies of knowledge about, for example, sociological theory, or research studies done, or particular sociologists' contributions, but this knowing is also knowing about application, about relevance, about judgement.

So, for example, I would invariably design a curriculum programme that begins by emphasising the essential character of the conceptual apparatus that sociologists, by different kinds, use in their analysis of social phenomena. What is characteristic about the sociological perspective, about the varied sociological points of view; the adequacy and inadequacy of all or some of these perspectives, *etc.* By definition, I always begin by indicating the shortcomings of sociology in understanding and explaining social reality, while going on to argue that sociology is undoubtedly better than anything else we have at our disposal!

Right from the outset of the delivery of the educational programme my intention is to lead the learners towards a position of independence from me; they become active knowers, practitioners in sociological analysis. This may well be only part of their becoming active knowers in a much broader or deeper practitioner-sense as well, but we all need to start somewhere.

It is certainly true that our 'knowledge-in-action' is underpinned by, is informed by, the theories we hold about the world and ourselves in it. Schon also comments on this:

> "... it is sometimes possible, by observing and reflecting on our actions, to make a description of the tacit knowing implicit in them. Our descriptions are of different kinds, depending on our purposes and the languages of description available to us. We may refer, for example, to the sequences of operations and procedures we execute; the clues we observe and the rules we follow; or the values, strategies, and assumptions that make up our 'theories' of action."

(Schon, 1987, p.25)

When I design a sociology curriculum for adults, I begin with my acknowledgement of their existing skills in managing the self and the social. They have, as adult members of society, already learnt, reflected upon, giving meaning to and adapted/modified, necessary skills for everyday life. In the course of these processes they have also developed a set of theories about the self and the social that underpin, even underwrite, their ideas, beliefs and action.

I see one of the values of sociology is in posing the question about the ideological inevitability of the existence of these 'personalised' theories. It is quite clear, of course, that the degree of self-consciousness that people have of their range of theories, and its relevance for their actions, varies enormously. I see one of my tasks (within a framework of a critical sociology) is to demonstrate the manner in which sociology offers alternative sets of theories and evidence in the pursuit of a fuller understanding of social phenomena.

Part of my strategy therefore has always been to draw-out from students, and make manifest, the sets of theories they have, while comparing and contrasting these to the range of sociological theories on offer. In this way, students not only have the opportunity to reflect upon their own theories of action (which can of course raise important biographical questions for them), they can also make judgements about the relative values to be placed upon other theories. In this way students can move from knowing to questioning to reflection on knowing and action that can excite their curiosity about the *unknown*, (*e.g.* the great wealth of sociological literature) without denying themselves as skilled social actors or denying the possibility for change.

It is worth making a distinction at this point between knowing-in-action and reflection-in-action.

> "In reflection-in-action, the rethinking of some part of our knowing-in-action leads to on-the-spot experiment and further thinking that affects what we do - in the situation at hand and perhaps also in others we shall see as similar to it.
>
> The distinction between reflection and knowing-in-action may be subtle. A skilled performer adjusts his responses to variations in phenomena. In this moment-by-moment appreciation of a process, he deploys a wide-ranging repertoire, of images of contexts and actions."
>
> *(Schon, op. cit., p.29)*

Let me reflect upon this sociologically by quoting from a piece of writing of my own and by making reference to Erwing Goffman who was always concerned with such issues:

> "Students of all kinds come to sociology, with, to say the least, a fascinating mixture of attitude and opinions about the subject (not to mention the subject matter). Any prospective teacher of sociology who does not acknowledge at the outset that he or she

is essentially part of this subject really misses the point. How is the sociologist's presentation going to affect the student - what effect is the teacher planning to make? Part of my concern with presentation is, just how self-conscious is, or should be, the sociologist as entertainer? It is self-evident that teachers of sociology are impresarios; they are 'putters-on' of things, but classroom strategies for the sociologist should go beyond this. How much do these teachers rely on a rigid script - how much do they extemporise - what allowance is made for spontaneity - how do they use their lexicon of sociological knowledge, expertise and imagination in the day-to-day interactions that comprise their classes or lectures."

(Astley, 1985)

And, further:

"... we do have problems with the privileged nature of our sociological knowledge, and I think we do have to be self-conscious about that. Who would admit to relishing the relative ease of resting in the lee of our privileged sociological knowledge, before once again setting course for a good buffeting on the high seas of teaching...

...I see sociological knowledge as a lexicon. We can use this lexicon of sociological knowledge at our disposal, say, as we might look at any painter's work. It is not just the idiosyncratics of selection of this colour or that shape, but also their juxtaposition and overall effect on our senses and sensibilities that make it distinctive, that makes it stand out, that makes it important and significant. From a sociologist's viewpoint this can, and should, turn the ordinary business of transmitting bodies of knowledge into something far more interesting and significant; an educational experience for the participants. Effect, of course, is a vexed question in education, let alone sociology, and yes, some of the entertainment is epiphenomena. However, if well-ordered, the experience for the participants will go beyond this and make an important contribution to the education of these persons; and again, I frequently notice in discussions how often we move very slowly towards the idea that somehow sociology might be good for a person's education. Again, that has always been important to me, and the way in which we adopt our role, I think, is important there."

(Astley, op. cit.)

Let me now turn to Goffman as promised. Even casual observation of my epistemology will confirm the influence on my thinking. Goffman's reflections are very much part of my knowledge taken into action and further contextualizes my practice strategies. He says:

" '. . .so the person who delivers a talk can meld himself into the occasion, by how, as a speaker, he extemporaneously or apparently extemporaneously embellishes his text using his text as a basis for a situationally, sensitive rendition, mingling the living and the read, and in consequences of the way he handles himself, he can render his subject matter something that his listeners feel they can handle...but a deeper understanding is to be drawn, an understanding that speaks to the ultimate claims that society makes upon a person who performs. What the audience will sense in an esteemed speaker, as intelligence, wit and charm, what the audience will impute to him as his own internally encompassed character, all this turns out to be generated through what he does to effectively put himself at the disposal of an occasion, and hence its participants, opening himself up to it and to them, counting the rest of himself as something to be subordinated for the purpose.' (Goffman, 1981)"

(Astley, op. cit.)

One of the definitive statements made by Goffman on these matters is to be found in his book *The Presentation of Self in Everyday Life*. The importance and relevance of Goffman's work dating from the 1950s cannot be overestimated and I would like to draw a brief taste of them here. He says, right at the beginning of the book:

". . .when an individual enters the presence of others, they commonly seek to acquire information about him or to bring into play information about him already possessed. They will be interested in his general socio-economic status, his conception of self, his attitude towards them, his competence, his trustworthiness, *etc*. Although some of this

> information seems to be sought almost as an
> end in itself."

(Goffman, 1959, p.13)

Then, as an aside, there is a problem for teachers:

> "There are usually quite practical reasons for
> acquiring it. Information about the individual
> helps to define the situation, enabling others
> to know in advance what he will expect of
> them and what they may expect of him.
> Informed in these ways, the others will know
> how best to act in order to call forth a
> desired response from him."

Goffman goes further; he is talking about the *situation* now,
he goes further and talks about the individual:

> "During the period in which the individual is
> in the immediate presence of the others, few
> events may occur which directly provide the
> others with the conclusive information they
> will need if they are to direct wisely their
> own activity. Many crucial facts lie beyond
> the time and place of interaction or lie
> concealed within it."

He then moves further to try and link the individual and
others into the situation:

> "Regardless of the particular objective which
> the individual has in mind and of his motive
> for having this objective, it will be in his
> interests to control the conduct of the
> others, especially their responsible treatment
> of him. This control is achieved largely by

91

influencing the definition of the situation which the others come to formulate, and he can influence this definition by expressing himself in such a way as to give them the kind of impression that will lead them to act voluntarily in accordance with his own plan."

(Goffman, op. cit. p.15).

So what I spend a lot of my time doing as a teacher in the classroom, as I reflect on my practice, is that I have certain problems about how I am going to orientate myself and my student, particularly if I am going to talk about things which are their 'property', and not, apparently, obviously, explicitly, my 'property' or my domain or my concern, my activity, and that if I want to say some of the things that I want to say because I am a bossy sociology teacher or whatever. If I want to try and take them from one step to another step in their understanding of what is going on in our society, in their lives, then I have to decide where *they* are and where *I* am. I have to try to formulate ways, as a teacher, whereby I can actually get them to draw on themselves, or on me, and to find some kind of space where we actually talk about the things that we need to talk about. This is clearly a transactional model and certainly a developed, theoretically informed part of my practice.

One further extract from Goffman will serve as an exemplary illustration of the arguments here about self-conscious reflection-in-practice:

"... belief in the part one is playing. When an individual plays a part he implicitly requests his observers to take seriously the impression that is fostered before them. They are asked to believe that the character they see actually possesses the attributes he appears to possess, that the task he performs will have the consequences that are implicitly claimed for it, and that, in general, matters are what they appear to be. In line with this, there is the popular view that the individual offers his performance and puts on his show 'for the benefit of other people'. It will be convenient to being a consideration of performance by turning the question around and looking at the individual's own belief in the impression of reality that he attempts to engender in those among whom he finds himself."

(Goffman, op. cit.)

So Goffman is saying to me that I should not only be concerned with just what they, the students, think of me, but what I think of them and what we all think of the situation. I suspect that this kind of situation for professional practitioners is fairly commonplace even if less self-consciously so on the part of some practitioners.

On the question of the relationship between the desired intuitiveness of the practitioner and the process to produce it, David Pannick, a Barrister and an academic touched on this in a recent newspaper article about the 'reform' of the legal profession:

"Great advocacy is impossible to define, difficult to describe and hard to teach. The greatest advocates enjoyed a simplicity, directness and brevity of approach" and "advocacy vitally depends on understanding and responding to the mood of the court."

(Pannick, 1989, Guardian, 14-4-89)

This is most definitely an interrelationship between theories about knowing-in-action and the presentation of self in everyday life.

Similar comments have consistently been made by the educators of professionals who have reflected upon their practice in relation to its aims and effectiveness. One of the key issues that I have addressed above is the question of knowledge, its usage and relevance.

> "... to be able to take one's subject to bits and to restructure it in many different ways, devising all manner of different problems to cultivate patterns of thought, is indeed to have mastery of one's subject. It shows mastery on many different planes.
>
> The point is that to be a professional teacher involves the ability to restructure one's subject using the student's construction of concepts. To do so is one essential ingredient of being student-centred as well as (not 'rather than') subject-centred. That is why this book is called *Professionalism and Flexibility for Learning*, not *Professionalism and Flexibility in Teaching*.
>
> However, that is not all a professional teacher needs to know. He does not need to know all the research literature on students, teaching, learning, assessment and so on; but he needs to know that is exists, where to find it, how to use it, and to have an attitude which recognises that it is relevant. In the same way that a doctor spends years acquiring a background in anatomy, physiology, biochemistry and so on, and then applies his knowledge in a multitude of techniques for discerning the needs of his

patients, for treating them, and for evaluating the effects of the treatment he gives
them, so a teacher needs some background
know-ledge to use a wide variety of
techniques, to understand his students, to
help them, to assess their progress, and to
evaluate his own performance.

These techniques are essential to the
craft of a professional teacher, but the art of
teaching is more than its craft. A teacher's
art lies in adapting and combining his
techniques in creative ways. Creativity is a
mark of good teaching. In this sense
teaching is an art requiring both knowledge
and skill. Like other arts, it develops by
informed appreciation and criticism. For this
reason it needs to be more open. Only then
can improvements be developed."

(Bligh, 1982, p.15)

Very similar comments have been made by Ernest House in
his essay 'Technology versus Craft'. I would direct the interested reader to the whole article on a ten year 'history' of
debates on educational innovation. Let me simply quote very
briefly from House to support my own arguments about skill
and craft as a relevant epistemological and practice base:

"A major distinction is whether one
considers teaching to be a craft or a technology. A craft is based on tacit knowledge
and experience. It is learned through
apprenticeship. A technology is based on
explicit knowledge and principles. It is
learned through formal means. Without

question, the majority of teachers view teaching as a craft born of long experience."

(House in Taylor, 1979, p.147)

In his use of technology, House adds a footnote:

"The difference between conceiving teaching as a technology or as a craft is also related to models of educational evaluation. Teaching as technology is related to evaluation models having an objectivist epistemology and utilitarian ethics. Teaching as craft is related to models having a subjectivist epistemology and institutionist ethics. The former yields explicit knowledge; the latter yields tacit knowledge."

(House, ibid.)

Schon makes the point that the practice of professionals is not usually measured in terms of knowledge, but its appropriate application. Effectiveness and competence are the key issues in relation to practice - but, Schon argues, considering wisdom, talent, intuition or artistry as aspects of practice are seen as vague, or symbolic interactionist fantasies! Besides anything else, they do not seem objective or factual enough skills or knowledges to actually teach to apprentice professionals (Schon, 1987). He adds to this point by emphasising the particularity of practice in addition to points made about the generality of professionals:

"Practitioners of a profession differ from one another, of course, in their subspecialities, the particular experiences and perspectives they bring to their work, and their styles of operation. But they also share a common body of explicit, more or less systematically organised professional knowledge and what Geoffrey Vickers has called an 'appreciative system' - the set of values, preferences, and norms in terms of which they make sense of practice situations, formulate goals and directions for action and determine what constitutes acceptable professional conduct.

A professional's knowing-in-action is embedded in the socially and institutionally structured context shared by a community of practitioners. Knowing-in-practice is exercised in the institutional settings particular to the profession, organised in terms of its characteristic units of activity and its familiar types of practice situations, and constrained or facilitated by its common body of professional knowledge and its appreciative system.

So much we can say without making explicit reference to a particular epistemology of professional practice. Beyond this point, however, our view of a practitioner's knowing will greatly affect our descriptions of the functions and interactions of professional knowledge and professional artistry."

(Schon, op. cit., p.33)

In this respect, discussions about professional competence go well beyond a concern with the rote learning of bodies of 'theoretical' knowledge of a technical rationality kind.

So professional practitioners do seem to operate on the basis of two distinguishable practice situations. Firstly, familiar situations where routine application of facts, rules and the procedures derived from a body of professional knowledge is used to solve problems. Secondly, there are invariably unfamiliar situations where a practitioner has not been taught a specific set of 'appropriate' responses. What is important and significant here is on what does the practitioner then draw to classify and deal with the problem? How self-conscious is this process and does the practitioner learn from and assimilate this situation?

Schon argues through this point as well:

> "In such cases, the practitioner experiences a surprise that leads her to rethink her knowing-in-action in ways that go beyond available rules, facts, theories, and operations. She responds to the unexpected or anomalous be restructuring some of her strategies of action, theories of phenomena, or ways of framing the problem; and she invents on-the-spot experiments to put her new understandings to the test. She behaves more like a researcher trying to model an expert system than like the 'expert' whose behaviour is modelled.
>
> Underlying this view of the practitioner's reflection-in-action is a constructionist view of the reality with which the practitioner deals - a view that leads us to see the practitioner as constructing situations of his practice, not only in the exercise of professional artistry, but also in all other modes of professional competence.
>
> Technical rationality rests on an objectivist view of the relation of the knowing practitioner to the reality he knows. On this view, facts are what they are, and the truth of beliefs is strictly testable by reference to them. All meaningful dis-agreements are

resolvable, at least in principle, by reference to the facts. And professional knowledge rests on a foundation of facts.

In the constructionist view, our perceptions, appreciations, and beliefs are rooted in worlds of our own making that we come to accept as reality. Communities of practitioners are continually engaged in what Nelson Goodman (1978) calls 'worldmaking'. Through countless acts of attention and inattention, naming, sense-making, boundary setting and control, they make and maintain the worlds matched to their professional knowledge and know-how. They are in transaction with their practice worlds, framing the problems that arise in practice situations and shaping the situations to fit the frames, framing their roles and constructing practice situations to make their role-frames operational. They have, in short, a particular, professional way of seeing their world and a way of constructing and maintaining the world as they see it. When practitioners respond to the indeterminate zones of practice by holding a reflective conversation with the materials of their situations, they remake a part of their practice world and thereby reveal the usually tacit processes of 'worldmaking' that underlie all of their practice."

(Schon, op. cit., p.35/36)

The Social Environment Needed for the Delivery of Reflective Practice Skills

I now want to turn, as promised, to what Schon calls the 'Practicum' (Schon, 1987). Schon draws on some fairly traditional and conventional sociological ideas about acculturation, socialisation, social control, structuration and role learning in his contextual remarks. He also, fairly conventionally, distinguishes between professional social-isation processes that are more or less solitary. Schon then turns to his definition:

> "A practicum is a setting designed for the task of learning a practice. In a context that approximates a practice world, students learn by doing, although their doing usually falls short of real-world work. They learn by undertaking projects that simulate and simplify practice; or they take on real-world projects under close supervision. The pra-cticum is a virtual world, relatively free of the pressures, distraction and risks of the real one, to which, nevertheless, it refers. It stands in an intermediate space between the practice world, the 'lay' world or ordinary life, and the esoteric world of the academy. It is also a collective world in its own right, with its own mix of materials, tools, languages and appreciations. It embodies particular ways of seeing, thinking and doing that tend, over time, as far as the student is concerned, to assert themselves with increasing authority.
>
> When a student enters a practicum, she is presented, explicitly or implicitly, with certain fundamental tasks. She must learn to

recognise competent practice. She must build an image of it, an appreciation of where she stands in relation to it, and a map of the path by which she can get from where she is to where she wants to be. She must come to terms with the claims implicit in the practicum: that a practice exists, worth learning, learnable by her, and represented in its essential features by the practicum. She must learn the 'practice of the practicum' - its tools, methods, projects and possibilities - and assimilate to it her emerging image of how she can best learn what she wants to learn."

(Schon, 1987, p.37/38)

There are definitely echoes of Goffman here and it certainly evokes for me ideas about 'a structure of feeling' put forward by Raymond Williams (1981).

Schon articulates the view that the student is at the centre of matters and that by implication one of the primary tasks of the teacher of professions is to construct, create and develop the practicum such that the appropriate and desired interactions take place.

"The work of the practicum is accomplished through some combination of the student's learning by doing, her interactions with coaches and fellow students, and a more diffuse process of 'background learning'.

Students practice in a double sense. In simulated, partial, or protected form, they engage in the practice they wish to learn. But they also practice, as one practices the piano, the analogues in their fields of the pianist's scales and arpeggios. They do these things under the guidance of a senior practitioner - a studio master, supervising physician, or case instructor, for example. From time to time, these individuals may teach in the conventional sense, communicating information, advocating theories, describing examples of practice. Mainly, however, they function as coaches whose main activities are demonstrating, advising, questioning and criticizing.

Most practicums involve groups of students who are often as important to one another as the coach. Sometimes they play the coach's role. And it is through the medium of the group that a student can immerse himself in the world of the practicum - the all-encompassing worlds of a design studio, a musical conservatory, or psychoanalytic supervision, for example - learning new habits of thought and action. Learning by exposure and immersion, background learning, often proceeds without conscious awareness, although a student may become aware of it later on, as he moves into a different setting.

Our view of the work of the practicum and the conditions and processes appropriate to it depends in part on our view of the kinds of knowing essential to professional competence."

(Schon, ibid.)

However, Schon keeps his options open about the character of the practicum. As I have reflected throughout this section, he attempts to relate questions about the social construction of professional education processes to the commonly held perspectives on knowledge.

> "If we see professional knowledge in terms of facts, rules, and procedures applied non-problematically to instrumental problems, we will see the practicum in its entirety as a form of technical training. It will be the business of the instructor to communicate and demonstrate the application of rules and operations to the facts of practice. One might imagine, on this view, a practicum for learning a computer language, techniques of analytic chemistry, or methods of statistical analysis. Students would be expected to acquire the material by reading, listening and watching, familiarising themselves with examples of practice problems matched to the appropriate categories of theory and techque. Coaching would consist in obsering student performance, detecting errors of application, pointing out correct responses.
>
> If we see professional knowing in terms of 'thinking like a' manager, lawyer, or teacher, students will still learn relevant facts and operations but will also learn the forms of inquiry by which competent practitioners reason their way, in problematic instances, to clear connections between general knowledge and particular cases. The standard drills of the law school classroom and the medical clinic exemplify this view. In a practicum of this kind, there is presumed to be a right answer for every situation, some item in the corpus of professional knowledge that can be seen, eventually, to fit the case

> at hand. But, depending on one's view of 'thinking like a _____' coaches may emphasise either the rules of inquiry or the reflection-in-action by which, on occasion, students must develop new rules and methods of their own."
>
> *(Schon, ibid.)*

These appropriate qualifications do remind us of the 'fit' or otherwise of professional knowledges to problems. If we see students as needing to acquire a form of reflection-in-action that goes beyond routine, stable rules which have probably been rote learnt, we are suggesting that students' competencies must include the ability to devise new methods of reasoning by constructing and testing new categories of understanding, strategies of action, and ways of problem framing. Now again there is nothing unique in this thinking. Schon is highlighting very commonplace sociological ideas about the definition of the situation. This would usually be formulated thus. The individual actor's assessment of the social situation she or he is in, which forms the basis of her/his interactions with other actors - that is, the process by which she/he refers the interaction and her/his role in it to her/his experience and understanding of other relevant situations.

It is also important here to remind ourselves that the competence of professional practitioners in the field incorporates - indeed, relies on, to a good measure - knowing-in-action that facilitates reflection-in-action. The theorising-in-action that takes place is almost certain to be beyond the capabilities of the student practitioner largely because of the contextual sheer depth of experience. The practicum should make use of the teacher's recognition of such to create learning environments and situations for the student that can and do act as exemplary illustrations of the skills and reflection on learning those skills. It is understandable therefore that those teachers who desire to develop a practicum along such lines will, for example, rely a good deal on students learning from each other.

At this point, it is worth recalling Brookfield's recent work on critical thinking and critical thinkers. In recognising critical thinking he suggests:

1. Critical thinking is a productive and positive activity
2. Critical thinking is a process, not an outcome
3. Manifestations of critical thinking vary according to the contexts in which it occurs
4. Critical thinking is triggered by positive as well as negative events
5. Critical thinking is emotive as well as rational.

Brookfield identifies the following as components of critical thinking:

1. Identifying and challenging assumptions is central to critical thinking
2. Challenging the importance of context is crucial to critical thinking
3. Critical thinkers try to imagine and explore alternatives
4. Imagining and exploring alternatives leads to reflective scepticism.

(Brookfield, 1987)

Further, I have no hesitation in quoting C. Wright Mills on *The Sociological Imagination*, the progenitor of so much else.

> "The sociological imagination enables its possessor to understand the larger historical scene in terms of its meaning for the inner life and the external career of a variety of individuals. It enables him to take into acc-

ount how individuals, in the welter of their daily experience, often become falsely conscious of their social positions. Within that welter the framework of modern society is sought, and within that framework the psychologies of a variety of men and women are formulated. By such means the personal uneasiness of individuals is focused upon explicit troubles and the indifference of publics is transformed into involvement with public issues.

The first fruit of this imagination - and the first lessons of the social science that embodies it - is the idea that the individual can understand his own experience and gauge his own fate only by locating himself within his period, that he can know his own chances in life only by becoming aware of those of all individuals in his circumstances. In many ways, it is a terrible lesson; in many ways, a magnificent one. We do not know the limits of man's capacities for supreme effort or willing degradation, for agony or glee, for pleasurable brutality or the sweetness of reason. But in our time we have come to know that the limits of 'human nature' are frighteningly broad. We have come to know that every individual lives, from one generation to the next, in some society; that he lives out a biography, and that he lives it out within some historical sequence. By the fact of his living he contributes, however minutely, to the shaping of this society and to the course of its history, even as he is made by society and by its historical push and shove." *(Mills, 1959, p.11/12)*

Mills goes on to focus on the interrelation between the tension between the individual and society that is now a commonplace aspect of most attempts to analyse the contexts in which the professional practitioner is developed and practices:

> "Perhaps the most fruitful distinction with which the sociological imagination works is between 'the personal troubles of milieu' and 'the public issues of social structure'. This distinction is an essential tool of the sociological imagination and a feature of all classic work in social science.
>
> Troubles occur within the character of the individual and within the range of his immediate relations with others; they have to do with his self and with those limited areas of social life of which he is directly and personally aware. Accordingly, the statement and the resolution of troubles properly lie within the individual as a biographical entity and within the scope of his immediate milieu - the social setting that is directly open to his personal experience and to some extent his wilful activity. A trouble is a private matter: values cherished by an individual are felt by him to be threatened.
>
> Issues have to do with matters that transcend these local environments of the individual and the range of his inner life. They have to do with the organisation of many such milieux into the institutions of a historical society as a whole, with the ways in which various milieux overlap and inter-penetrate to form the larger structure of social and historical life. An issue is a public

107

matter: some value cherished by publics is felt to be threatened. Often there is a debate about what the value really is and about what it is that really threatens it. This debate is often without focus if only because it is the very nature of an issue, unlike even widespread trouble, that it cannot very well be defined in terms of the immediate and everyday environments of ordinary men. An issue, in fact, often involves a crisis in institutional arrangements, and often too it involves what Marxists call 'contradictions' or 'antagonisms'."

(Mills, op. cit., p.14/15)

So as to illustrate this point further with a very representative example, let me quote from Mike Simpkin:

"I suggest...that social work is a fundamentally ambiguous and conflict-ridden activity which it is difficult to define or describe in a way which outsiders can easily understand. Eager to please, we are rarely able to satisfy one party, let alone all; we work in an emotional hothouse of guilt, blame and recrimination. Our material and methods are not quantifiable and we can rarely decisively control the factors which could lead our work to a successful outcome. Furthermore, the pressure we are under combines with the personal traits which have led many of us into social work anyway to make us highly defensive not only against outside criticism but even against each other - divisions which are reinforced by the highly individualistic tradition of our theory and

practice. Our strongest defence is to concentrate upon 'client' behaviour. The very
use of such a term suggests a realm worthy
of detailed and separate attention, though I
shall use 'client' throughout the book for
convenience; alternatives are equally inaccu-
rate and unilluminating. (It is the role which
has to be changed; the terminology will
follow.) By spending so much of our time
purporting to understand clients, we are
largely able to ignore our own actions and
reactions, and the effect they have on all
those who have to do with us, including each
other. Our own behaviour appears to fall into
some separate category. We talk about the
use of self, but lack of self-awareness is
common to all the helping professions; that
too is a product of our role. Still the blatant
social incompetence and insensitivity of
many social workers and psychiatrists is
astonishing among people who pretend to
some expertise in relationships."

(Simpkin, 1979, p.1/2)

Social work, like many other 'people work' professions, has
come a long way since the late 1970s. It would, however, be
naïve in the extreme to suggest that these professions have
grasped the reasons, necessity or skills, for, having a
sociological imagination, critical thought, or reflective
practice!

These concerns echo quite self-consciously the concerns
outlined in my Introduction to this essay. It was there that I
argued that my long-term concern was to focus on the
curriculum of professional education; but, then to sharpen
my focus through reflection upon my response to the

debates on and around the concepts of reflective practice and the reflective practitioner. My research is from the standpoint of a critical and reflexive sociology, which heightens the role of theory while outlining the possibilities for doing empirical work to generate data on related phenomena to professional education. It is essential to recognise here that for me my practice as both sociologist and teacher places demands and requirements to theorise. My reflective practice is very largely the 'nitty gritty' of this essay, the theoretically generated philosophical debates of the issues and arguments involved. The main advocates for the development of reflective practice argue that changes must take place within professional education to implement this fundamental reorientation. However, it should be added that to make changes within the structure of professional education alone, an island of radicalism within a sea of conservatism, would be difficult to carry off to say the least. Most experiences of innovation in the curriculum emphasise the difficulty in 'swimming against the stream' even when there is a climate generally favourable to change. The present epoch of educational reform may be viewed by some as radical, *i.e.* it is part of the overall pattern in government led policy making to discard the social democratically informed welfare corporatist approaches of the post_War years. Moreover that radicalness has rested heavily on a technical rationality at best and an irrational authoritarianism at worst. The climate for curriculum innovation of a non-technicist kind is not a marked feature of the 1980s.

So on the one hand we have a demand for change:

> "Current trends in policy and practice are making new and far-reaching demands on nursing education; and teachers of nursing and their schools and colleges are under considerable pressure to improve their courses, at every level. It is probably in part

> as a response to these demands that the nursing education world has recently become interested in theoretical and practical developments in curriculum design in the wider world of education."
>
> *(Beattie, 1987)*

On the other hand, we have the sets of constraints experienced by many professional educators and innovators. One of the most potent forces for the status quo is the real difficulty of carrying the innovations into the real workplace of the great bulk of the profession in question. There are problems with resources both human and material. It is one thing to acknowledge a conventional wisdom that education or training takes place in the workplace; that all professionals in supervisory roles have an educative role. But, does this professional socialisation actually happen in a systematic way and aim to achieve educational goals devised as part of the innovatory strategy?

> "We often hear that ward sisters have a teaching role, but, this is nothing new. As long ago as 1879, the ward sister was said to train: 'the probationer nurses in their ward work both by direct instruction and by working with them.' Nevertheless, the importance attached to the educative role, and the ways in which teaching and learning occur, have been the focus of increased attention.
>
> Although my own studies have covered the preparation of ward sisters and the professional development of newly registered nurses, they both highlighted the sisters' educative role...

Looking back, the picture in the 1950s, the sixties and early seventies was often gloomy. For example, in 1953, Goddard found that teaching had a low priority for trained staff, that sisters only spent between 5% and 10% of their day in direct contact with students and that formal teaching comprised only 1.1% of their time. (Almost inevitably, this involved teaching students and little mention was made of their responsibility for teaching trained staff.) Government reports in the 1960s supported this. For example, one small study found that sisters spent less than 4% of their time teaching, and the Scottish Home and Health Department estimated that teaching averaged 15 minutes a day.

This did not necessarily mean that sisters were disinterested in teaching; a number of studies have found a discrepancy between their views on the ideal teaching role and the low priority they actually gave to ward teaching."

(Lathlean, 1987)

Some critics within nursing would go even further in suggesting that nurse teachers in general are a long way from an epistemology that is likely to be innovative in direct relation to the improvement of patient care.

"The 'view of the world' within which nursing education is inherently embedded is Western liberalism; thus nursing education has evolved within the context of a society with a strong individualistic transition. Western liberalism has also produced the contemporary ideology of *Social Atomism* (Wolgast, 1980), an ideology that is an insufficient social context for education for health care... Reviewing the philosophies of education pertaining to different colleges of nursing... the most striking commonality is the premise that education must be centrally concerned with the growth and development of the individual person. On this view nursing education is not primarily concerned with creating a certain kind of health care, sensitive to the health care needs of society, but rather its primary duty is the promotion of the autonomous individual. The concept of autonomy is, therefore, set within the structure of nursing education's social and educational values, but its conceptual characteristics do not have any necessary implications for the development of a positive commitment to others, in terms of care, concern and compassion. This, however, is not to suggest that writers outside of nursing education have failed to recognise this void - merely that nurse teachers are forced to adopt a paradoxical position and certainly one that is incongruent with education for health care."

(Glen, 1988)

Schon and others argue for the establishment of a flexible reflective practicum that can coach 'students' in the ways of reflective practice. Confidence, strong role-modelling, and a commitment to the quest as a whole are clearly essential. But, as I have already indicated, pressures exist both outside and inside the 'schools' of professional education. Not the least of the strains in evidence is the tension between

Professionalism and Managerialism that has surfaced on many occasions in this essay, as well as in many other discussions of these issues. (Balogh and Beattie, 1988; refer also Christman on education standards and Kramer on education preparation for nurse roles, in Williamson, 1976).

Much of the above raises questions about encouraging critical thinking or reflective practice in the workplace. Argyris, with and without Schon, has developed the idea of double-loop learning (Argyris, 1976, 1982 and Argyris and Schon, 1974, 1978).

Essentially, professionals use double-loop learning to identify, question and change the assumptions underlying the organisation of the workplace and the patterns of interaction that are typical. An essential aspect of this process is the attempt by practitioners in any workplace to recognise aspects of the organisational culture and various sub-cultures that stand in the way of change and are actually injurious to productivity, morale and communication.

> "Perhaps the clearest guidelines on how to assist people to become double-loop learners are contained in Argyris (1976, 1982). Argyris is particularly interested in the nested paradoxes evident in executives' reasoning. Nested paradoxes are forms of reasoning that lead to productive cons-equences in the short term and unproductive consequences in the long term. Each stage in the executive's reasoning process is iden-tified, and the feelings accompanying its accomplishment are described. Executives are encouraged to write out scenarios of how they have solved work-related problems and then to analyse what they have written as if they were trying to help a friend. Skilled

helpers then point out the contradictions between feelings and actions."

(Brookfield, 1987, p.158)

In many respects this brings me back to Argyris' and Schon's unequivocal statement that a central concern with practice must be the main aim of professional education, or if you like, the 'integration of practice into professional education'.

It has become a cliché to say that the professional must 'relate knowledge to effective action,' or 'integrate theory and practice'; however, it is not agreed that the professional school should effect this integration.

There are three perspectives on the relationships among basic theory, theory of practice, and skills that lead to sharp disagreement on which tasks are appropriate to the school and which to the office.

One school of thought regards theory of practice as deriving from basic theory and as testable without recourse to practice...

...This school of thought holds that teaching about practice is a diversion from the essential academic tasks; the school should develop and convey basic theory relevant to professional practice, and the office should provide opportunity to acquire professional skills.

A second school of thought comes to the same conclusion by a different route. Some professionals and educators advance the notion that effective practice involves intuitive knowledge that is not amenable to explicit formulation, even in principle. This is the position of the adherent of professional mystique - a position that is found in all professions. This kind of professional knows that he knows something, knows that students do not know it, knows that he cannot tell others what he knows, but knows that they should come to know it. How then do they come to know it? In mysterious ways, perhaps by a kind of osmosis, through proximity to a master - as in apprentice-ship....

The adherent of professional mystique also believes that the intuitive knowledge central to professional skills must be acquired in practice.

These two points of view may be merged: the profe-ssional school is responsible for developing basic theory that leads to the best technique, and practice is responsible for teaching, in some mysterious way, how to apply theory and technique effectively.

The third school of thought says that the professional school should teach the student to think like a professional."

(Argyris and Schon, 1974, p.183/4)

Argyris and Schon argue that each of these paradigms is flawed. On the first point, they say:

"...given a theory of practice, we may support or criticise its assumptions by referring to basic theory, yet in the absence of a theory of practice, we can be reasonably sure of the pertinence of a particular basic theory to professional competence only if we can be reasonably sure that some of the assumptions in a theory of practice are basic assumptions of that particular kind. This presumption is more feasible for some professions than for others."

(Argyris and Schon, ibid., p.185)

On the second point, they argue: what use is basic theory if it cannot be realised in effective practice? They also want to stress that the practitioner's actions in reality are not mysteriously unrelated to what knowledges are acquired.

Their third point is that learning to be a professional practitioner actually requires building one's own theory of practice which of necessity refocuses attention on the need of the learner to be engaged in practice situations.

Argyris and Schon place a considerable amount of importance upon the access, which learners need, must have, to practice. They emphasise that simulation and field experience are the typical ways in which the student profession has access to practice situations. Argyris and Schon share a common concern with other writers about the value of experiential learning. David Kolb has been one of the more prolific writers on this (1984) and the collection of essays edited by Kolb, Rubin and McIntyre (1979) all focus on these contextual concerns about the social and psychological environment of learning for adults. Despite their acknowledgement of the increased value placed upon fieldwork by professional educators, Argyris and Schon express doubts about the usefulness of this practice experience for students. For example, they argue that educationally, the meaning of fieldwork has remained unclear:

> "In our opinion, the field experience should not be designed simply to give students

experience, it is not enough. The school is obligated to offer more to the student; otherwise, the student finds himself paying tuition fees to learn something for which he does not need a faculty's help and that he could be paid to learn if he took a job and began to work....

The objective of the field experience, like the objective of all clinical experience, is to learn to become more reflective under real-time conditions so that effective *ad hoc* theories of action can be created and tested.

Insofar as clinical experience is intended to help the student learn to build his own theory of practice, the real or simulated situations of practice ought to have different characteristics depending on the functions to be filled."

(Argyris and Schon, op.cit., p.188)

In concluding this section, I must return to some very basic questions about the establishment and design of a curriculum for professional education that can, in fact, be delivered in a committed and coordinated way by educators and students alike.

One of the key issues for me is quite essentially what is to form the core of the curriculum, which can support the promotion of reflective practice? There are certainly two conventional approaches here, which have been the subject of my discussion throughout this essay in relation to the questions about what constitutes professional knowledge. On the one hand, many professional educators argue that the core curriculum must be the conceptual apparatus that is necessary for the professional practitioner. Students must learn a set of analytical skills that can, as soon as possible, make them 'independent' of their teachers. Teaching students how to think for themselves as practitioners is another way of putting it.

Secondly, there are those professional educators who insist on the transmission of a body of technical, practice-orientated, knowledge and skills that must be known. This second viewpoint is often articulated in a way that seems to be suggesting that whether these knowledges are actually to be used/practised or not is irrelevant. It is almost as if students need to be exposed to them, like radiation, and they will be given a lasting and relevant dose!

I find myself more inclined towards the first option, the conceptual core, while being only too well aware that a good deal of any core must be associated with, at least, a body of conventional professional knowledge - for example, the 'literature' of the profession.

However, it is quite obvious that it is essential to create a learning situation where students learn the skills of accessing information - the 'literature' say - when they need it. It is also absolutely essential to encourage in students the belief that there is a very high value to be placed upon acquiring and using such skills. In my experience, students of all kinds, from many different professions, including sociology, acknowledge the importance of being skilled for independence, but still find it difficult to disassociate themselves from the belief that the most important knowledge must be handed down to them on 'tablets of stone' by their teachers.

I see no alternative to the establishment in the 'practicum' of a learning environment that stresses the independence of the student. However, this does not mean students are abandoned by their teachers. On the contrary, the commitment to reflective practice includes a judgement by all those involved that this is a cooperative activity to which different actors contribute valuable aspects of the learning experience.

Schon and others have used the term 'coaching' a good deal and I like this idea; largely perhaps because I have been doing it for a long time! In an important way it refers back directly to my arguments in the Introduction to this essay about the design of an organic curriculum in relation to knowledge and human interests.

My recent experience of course planning for degree courses in Nursing and Midwifery have confirmed many of my hopes and fears in these respects. I am very sceptical about what I see as a good deal of 'fellow travelling', 'bandwagon riding' or whatever, embracing of reflective practice by people who clearly have not thought it through. It is inevitable that innovatory ideas are attractive to professionals when they are casting around for support in relation to change. However, despite the degree of care that was put into the designing of these new Nursing and Midwifery courses a lot of problems remain unresolved. An enormous amount of time and energy was devoted to the designing of the core curriculum and as a social scientist, I was directly involved in this aspect of course design. What has emerged, however, is very similar to the compromises between conceptual frameworks and technical knowledges that dominate the curriculum of other, older, courses of professional education that I teach on.

I do not have any doubts that students coming to these new courses will be intrigued, enthused and overwhelmed. It is one thing to say to students, be an independent learner, be a reflective practitioner, and another reality for the student to cope adequately in the constraints of time and space. It is assumed that the curriculum which incorporates reflective practice is liberating rather than domesticating. The proof, however, may rest with whether the 'academic' demands and clinical practice competence conventions placed upon students will get in the way? It would not be difficult to envisage a situation where even given a curriculum with reflective practice at its heart that students under pressure will opt in an instrumental way for the extrinsic, rather than intrinsic, values of their educational experience. I do have a lingering doubt about the ability of many professional educators to liberate themselves via reflective practice. If professional educators are merely tokenistic in their ill-informed embracing of reflective practice, I can see little change taking place in the educational experiences of students.

Conclusion

I do not have much more to add. My interest in both the concept of reflective practice and the debates about its application has increased as a consequence of researching for, and writing, this essay. My numerous discussions with people, regardless of their degree of access to the literature, have proved invaluable to sharpening up my own conceptions and perceptions.

I remain an enthusiastic advocate of reflective practice. I even remain committed to its incorporation into courses of education for professionals. I am still sceptical about both the motives of some protagonists and their ability and that of others to successfully translate the rhetoric into an educational experience that is meaningful and relevant for all.

I have researched and written this essay from my perspective as a sociologist and more specifically as a 'critical' social theorist. In this context, I am fundamentally concerned with the questions of action and change. I have entitled this essay 'The New Professionals?' as an indication of both my awareness of developments, and caution, about the whole project. This is not to argue for delay, to hold back on the development of the curriculum, which includes a commitment to reflective practice. On the contrary, I am in favour of a bold approach to adoption, design, development and delivery now. But adoption, *etc.*, will also mean adaptation and a great deal of this will rely upon the intuition and artistry of the reflective practitioners engaged in the task.

I do not doubt that nursing, like other 'people-work' and occupational groups are striving to improve and/or enhance their status. I am in no doubt at all that a major motive for redesigning educational programmes, especially at first-degree level, is to raise the status of various professions. However, there is no guarantee at all that nursing, or other professional groups, will change for the better in terms of service or care delivered. Indeed, unless many of the educational changes on offer are handled with the utmost care, any of these professions could produce hybrid creations of self-interested individuals worthy Doctor Frankenstein!

I hope that the reader has enjoyed this essay. I also hope that any readers who have the time and the inclination will take up the issues in debate, both during and after the educational programmes we might tend to focus our attention upon.

BIBLIOGRAPHY
ALLAN, P. and JOLLEY, M. (eds) *The Curriculum in Nursing Education*, Beckenham, Croom Helm, 1987
ARGYRIS, C. *Personality and Organisation - The Conflict between System and the Individual*, New York, Harper & Row, 1957
ARGYRIS, C. and SCHÖN, D. A. *Theory in Practice: Increasing Professional Effectiveness*, Jossey-Bass Inc., San Francisco, 1974
ARGYRIS, C. and SCHÖN, D. A. *Organisational Learning: A Theory of Action*, Addison-Wesley, NY, 1978
ARMSTRONG, D. 'The way we teach Medical Sociology' in Gomm, R., and McNeill, P., 1982
ASTLEY, J. 'The Sociology Teacher as Entertainer' in Lambe and Joseph, 1985
ATKINSON, P. *Language, Structure and Reproduction. An Introduction to the Sociology of Basil Bernstein*, Methuen, London, 1985
AUSUBEL, D. P. (ed.) *Educational Psychology: a cognitive view*, Holt, Rinehart & Winston, New York, 1978
BALOGH, R. and BEATTIE, A. *Performance Indicators in Nursing Education*, Final Report on a Feasibility Study. U.L.I.E., 1988

BAUMAN, Z. *Socialism, the active Utopia*, London, Allen & Unwin, 1976

BEATTIE, A. 'Making a Curriculum Work', in Allan and Jolley, 1987

BECKER, H. S., *et al* (eds.) *Institution and the Person*, Aldine Publishing Co., Chicago, 1968

BENNETT, W. S. and HOKENSTAD, M. C. 'Full time People Workers and conceptions of the Professional', in Halmos, 1973

BERGER, P. *Facing up to Modernity*, Harmondsworth, Penguin, 1979

BLIGH, D. (ed.) *Professionalism and flexibility in Learning*, Guildford, S.R.H.E. Monograph, 1982

BRAVERMAN, H. *Labour and Monopoly Capital*, New York, Monthly Review Press, 1974

BROOKFIELD, S. D. *Developing Critical Thinkers*, Milton Keynes, Open University Press, 1987

BRUNER, J. S. *Research Program on Intellectual Development*, Cambridge, Harvard Univ. Press, 1969

BUCKER, R. and STRAUSS, A. 'Professions in Process', *American Journal of Sociology* 66, Jan. 1961.

CLARKE, M. 'Action and Reflection: Practice and Theory in Nursing', *Journal of Advanced Nursing*, 11(1) p.3-11, 1986

COOPER, C. L. (ed.) *Theories of Group Processes*, London, Wiley, 1975

COULSON-THOMAS, C. 'Can Professions adapt and survive?' *Sunday Telegraph*, 5 March 1989.

CROSS, K. P. *Accent on Learning: Improving Instruction, Reshaping the Curriculum*, San Francisco, Jossey-Bass, 1976

DAVIS, B. D. (ed.) *Research into Nurse Education*, London, Cross Helm, 1983

DAVIS, B. D. (ed.) *Nursing Education: Research and Development*, Croom Helm, London, 1987

DAVID, F. 'Professional Socialisation as Subjective Experience: The Process of Doctrinal Conversion amongst student nurses', in Becker, 1968

DEWEY, J. *How We Think: A Restatement of the Relation of Reflective Thinking to the Educative Process*, Chicago, Henry Regnery, 1933

DINGWALL, R. AND LEWIS, P. (eds.) *The Sociology of the Professions*, London, Macmillan, 1983

DOWIE, J. and ELSTEIN, D. (eds.) *Professional Judgement*, Cambridge, CUP, 1988

ESLAND, G. (ed.) *People and Work*, Edinburgh, Holmes McDougall and Open University Press, 1977

FOUCALT, M. *Archaeology of Knowledge*, pub.Tavistock, London, 1974

FRIEDSON, E. *Profession of Medicine. A Study of the Sociology of Applied Knowledge*, University of Chicago, 1970

FRIEDSON, E *Professional Powers. A Study of the Institutionalisation of Formal Knowledge*, University of Chicago, 1988

GAGNE, R. M. *The Conditions of Learning*, Holt, New York, 1977

GALLIE, D. *Employment in Britain*, Oxford, Blackwell, 1989

GITLIN, A. and TEITELBAUM, K. 'Linking Theory and Practice: The Use of Ethnographic Methodology by Prospective Teachers', *Journal of Education for Teaching*, 9(3), p.225-34, 1983

GLEN, S. 'Do Nurse Teachers really want to Educate for care?' (1988) From unpublished MA Thesis, 'Nursing Moral Education for the 3 C's: Care, Concern and Correction', U.L.I.E. (1982).

GOFFMAN, E. *The Presentation of Self in Everyday Life*, Harmondsworth, Penguin, 1959

GOLDTHORPE, J. *Social Mobility and Class Structure in Modern Britain*, Oxford, Clarendon Press, 1987

GOMM, R. and MCNEILL, P. (eds.) *Handbook for Sociology Teachers*, Heinemann, London, 1982

GOODE, W. J. *Exploration in Social Theory*, The Free Press, New York, 1973

GOODMAN, J. Reflection and Teacher Education: A Case Study and Theoretical Analysis, Interchange, 15(3) p.9-25, 1984

GOULDNER, A. *The Coming Crisis of Western Sociology*, London, Heinemann, 1971

GRANT, C. A. (ed.) *Preparing for Reflective Teaching*, London, Allyn, 1984

GREAVES, F. Nurse Education and the Curriculum. A Curricular Model, Croom Helm, London 1984

HABERMAS, J. *Knowledge and Human Interests*, London, Heinemann, 1978

HALMOS, P. (ed.) *Professionalisation and Social Change*, Sociological Review Monograph, No.20, 1973

HALMOS, P. The Personal and the Political - Social Work and Political Action, Hutchinson, London, 1978

HELLER, A. *The Theory of Need in Marx*, Allison and Busby, London, 1976

HENDERSON, M. S. (ed.) *Nursing Education* (Recent advances in nursing 4), Edinburgh, Churchill-Livingstone, 1982

HIRST, P. and WOOLLEY, P. *Social Relations and Human Attributes*, London, Tavistock, 1982

HOLMES, J. *Professionalisation - a misleading myth?* N.Y.B., Leicester, 1981

HOUSE, E. 'Technology versus craft', in Taylor, 1979

HUGHES, E. (c. 1963) 'Professions' in *Daedalus*, Vol. 92, No.4, Autumn, 1973.

HUGHES, E., et *al Education for the Professions*, New York, McGraw-Hill, 1973

HUMPHRIES, B. 'Adult Learning in Social Work Education: towards liberation or domestication', in *Critical Social Policy*, Issue 23, Vol. 8, No. 2, Autumn, 1988.

ILLICH, I. *Disabling Professions*, London, M. Boyars, 1977

JACKSON, P. and MARSDEN, D. *Education and the Working Class*, Harmondsworth, Penguin, 1962

JARVIS, P. *Professional Education*, London, Croom Helm, 1983

JOHNSON, T. *Professions and Power*, London, Macmillan, 1972

KEDDIE, N. Adult Education: an ideology of individualism in Thompson, 1980

KILMINSTER, R. *Praxis and Method*, London, RKP, 1979

KNOWLES, M. The Adult Learner: A Forgotten Species, Croom Helm, London, 1973

KNOWLES, M. 'Androgogy: an emerging technology for Adult Learning' in Tight, 1983

KOLB, D. A. and FRY, R. 'Towards an Applied Theory of Experimental Learning' in Cooper, C. L. (ed.), 1975

KOLB, D. A., ROBIN, I. M. and MCINTYRE, J. M. *Organisational Psychology - A Book of Readings*, Prentice-Hall, Engleood Cliffs, New Jersey, 1979

KOLB, D. A. *Experimental Learning, Experience as the Source of Learning and Development*, Englewood Cliffs, Prentice-Hall, New Jersey, 1984

LAMBE, K., and JOSEPH, M. (eds.) *Teaching Sociology to non-Sociologists*, Oxford School of Business, 1985

LATHLEAN, J. 'The Ward Sister:Training the Teacher', in *Nursing Times*, Vol.83, No.49, 7 October 1987.

LEONARD, P. *Personality and Ideology*, London, Macmillan,1984

LAW, M. and RUBENSON, K. *Andragogy: The Return of the Jedi*, in S.C.U.T.R.E.A., 1988

MACINTYRE, A. *After Virtue: A study in moral theory*, London, Duckworth, 1981

MCEVOY, P. 'Prepare for Project 2000' in *Nursing Times*, Vol.85, No.6, 8 February 1989, p.40-1, 1989

MCGUIRE, J. *Threshold to Nursing*, London, Bell, 1969

MCILROW, J. 'A Critical Theory of Adult Learning and Education in Adult Education', Vol.32, No.1, Washington. 1981

MILLERSON, G. *The Qualifying Associations: A study of professionalisation*, London, RKP, 1984

MILLS, C. W. *The Sociological Imagination*, Harmondsworth, Penguin, 1959

NARR, W. D. *Pluralistiche Gesellschaft* (Pluralist Associations), Gessell, Hanover, 1969

NEAL, D. 'The First Year of a CQSW Course' in Gomm and McNeill, 1982.

O'NEILL, J. *Sociology as a Skin Trade*, London, Heinemann, 1972

PANNICK, D. 'Reforming the Legal Profession', *The Guardian*, 14 April 1989.

PEARSON, G. *The Deviant Imagination Psychiatry*, Social Work and Social Change, London, Macmillan, 1975

POLLARD, A. and TANN, S. *Reflective Teaching in the Primary School*, London, Cassell, 1987

RAYBOULD, E. (ed.) *A Guide for Teachers of Nurses*, Oxford, Blackwell, 1975

SCHÖN, D. A. *The Reflective Practitioner: How Professionals Think in Action, London*, Temple Smith, 1983

SCHÖN, D. A. *Educating the Reflective Practitioner, Toward a New Design for Teaching and Learning*, Jossey-Bass, London, 1987

SCUTREA: The papers from the Transatlantic Dialogue, Leeds Conference, July 1988.

SHOTTER, J. *Social Accountability and Selfhood*, Blackwell. Oxford, 1984

SIMPKIN, M. *Trapped within Welfare*, London, Macmillan, 1979

SMITH, J. P. *Sociology and Nursing*, Edinburgh, Churchill-Livingstone, 2nd edition, 1981

TAYLOR, P. H. (ed.) *New Directions in Curriculum Studies*, Brighton, Falmer Press, 1979

THOMPSON, J. L. (ed.) *Adult Education for a Change*, Hutchinson, London, 1980

TIGHT, M. (ed.) Education for Adults Vol.1, Adult Learning in Education, Croom Helm, London, 1983

WALKER, A. and WESTERGAARD, J. *Cross Currents in Views of Welfare: Prospects for Socialist Change*. Unpublished (1987) – also paper to Socialism and Social Policy Conference, Leeds Polytechnic, 1988.

WATSON, T. J. *The Personnel Managers, a study in the sociology of work and employment*, London, RKP, 1977

WEBB, C. (ed.) *Women's Health: Midwifery and Gynaecological Nursing*, London, Hodder & Stoughton, 1986

WILLIAMS, R. *Culture*, Glasgow, Fontana, 1981

WILLIAMSON, J. A. (ed.) *Current Perspectives in Nursing Education. The Changing Scene*, Saint Louis, The C. V. Mosby Company, 1976

WORSLEY, P. *Introducing Sociology*, Harmondsworth, Penguin, 1977

YOUNG, M. *The Rise of the Meritocracy*, Harmondsworth, Penguin, 1958

YOUNG, M. F. D. (ed.) *Knowledge and Control*, London, Collier Macmillan, 1971

ZEICHNER, K. M. 'On Becoming a Reflective Teacher' in Grant, C. A. (ed.) *Preparing for Reflective Teaching*, 1984

ZEICHNER, K. M. *Journal of Education for Teaching*, Vol.12, No.1, p.5-24, 1986

ZEICHNER, K. M. and TEITELBAUM, K. 'Personalised and Inquiry Oriented Teacher Education: An Analysis of Two Approaches to the Development of Curriculum for Field-based Experiences', *Journal of Education for Teaching*, 8(2), p.95-117, 1982

The University Lecturer as Research-Minded Practitioner

(2006 & 1999)

While still working full-time in H.E. in Oxford in the late 1980s, early 1990s, I became increasingly interested in the complex issues around learning and teaching within this professional practice. Of course I was regularly engaged in curriculum design for my own degree courses, and often (I am pleased to say) in collaboration with one or more colleagues for other, usually cross-departmental curricula. But I was also involved in cross institution teams designing much more wide ranging curriculum developments, for example, courses for professional practitioners. As a Sociologist, I found these various activities kept bringing me back to questions about professional roles; how are people prepared for them, what sets of values and cultural rules are they inculcated into, what do practitioners understand as ideal role performance trajectories and how does all this (and more) square with the institution that employs them?

At that time, I had planned to do much more work on this subject. Then, a while later, when I moved to the South West of England in 1996, I became involved in several pieces of consultancy for local universities. One of these tasks was to help coordinate a university-wide project on student-centred learning. The senior management of this particular institution, like so many others, felt that they needed to address a number of converging factors that did, or soon would, affect their curriculum offer. A good deal of pressure had come from Central Government; institutions of H.E. were to be reformed, standardised and made much more responsive to efficiency, effectiveness and value for money within 'the market economy' criteria. Resources were increasingly tight, and student-centred learning was seen, by some, as one way of spreading those resources under greater conditions of control: teachers should do less face-to-face work with students, while the latter should take on more explicit responsibility for their own learning. After all, all teachers need learners, but not all learners need teachers! Plus: this was all to be done while maintaining standards, with no diminution of the curriculum on offer.

And so I became involved in this two year long 'project' that sought to refocus university staff attention on the familiar territory of designing, delivering and evaluating a curriculum. I wrote a number of documents, and reports, even a regular newsletter, for staff consumption. I also wrote the piece that follows, the aim of which was to set the project specific issues within a wider context. All professional cultures, including those of academia, are notoriously difficult to change. The State soon loses patience with professionals, of all kinds, in the latter's attempts to reform from within the culture, and sets about forcing changes through control and compliance measures, including policy and funding. I offer this brief piece as an example of the many and various engagements made with these issues.

THE STUDENT CENTRED LEARNING (SCL) INITIATIVE: THE NEED FOR SOME THEORISING (1999)

Most colleagues are now familiar with the aims and objectives of SCL. Certainly many people will have become aware of the current issues around learning, teaching and curriculum change. Through talking to people I have noticed that, on the one hand many colleagues are 'new initiative weary', and yet very aware of the consequences of changes in university life that have a bearing on us all. The way we all practice is clearly at the centre of most people's thoughts and whatever reservations we may have about SCL as an initiative, it is undeniable that this myriad of issues is on our individual and collective agendas.

One of the *objectives* identified for the Initiative by the Universities senior management was:

"Facilitate and encourage institution-wide debate on the implications of student-centred learning for the subject, discipline or support area, and in particular to consider its potential impact on the curriculum, the structure and delivery of academic programmes and research."

This 'debate' is already underway, that much is clear, but what is not so explicit is the role of theorising within, and for, this debate. We are, after all, working within, contributing to, a network of social relations, and organisation, that values theory and theorists. Hopefully we also value theorising, which, as a social theorist, I have always considered to be a/the(?) key role. As reflective practitioners we are only too well aware of the diverse nature of our roles and the nature of interfaces with others. Most colleagues I talk to do regard themselves as research-minded practitioners, *i.e.*, where the value of theorising is at the heart of their day-to-day practice: where research is like an intellectual journey, where we do constantly consider and evaluate our motives, aims, objectives, success at achieving what we claim, and so on. We are also aware of the danger of 'packing our bags' for these journeys, but never actually making them!' Part of the difficulty here is the disparity between the theories related to our practice as a [whatever] that we espouse, and our actual theory in practice. . .

Those of us engaged in teaching also have a further prevailing problem in that we have to juggle with a dual practice. We are practitioners in our academic discipline, in my case Sociology, but we are also practitioners of education. Even at the most basic level these practices, disciplines, academic and education, are not one and the same. For example, the current body of knowledge paradigms are invariably separate, and very likely to be underpinned by fundamentally different theories of human action, and of research methodologies. So, to acknowledge these differences is the beginning of an intellectual, and essentially research focused journey. We all make these journeys, deliberately or not, voluntarily or not, with an explicit recognition of these processes, or not! Over many years, I have noticed that *academic* colleagues are proud to demonstrate their up-to-date-ness in their own discipline, and so they should. However, I have also been regularly struck by the out-of-touch-ness (not just not up-to-date) of colleagues when education as a practice is discussed. It has even been the case where very able theorists have boasted of never ever having read a book on education theory!

Now, I am certainly not saying that it is impossible to be a competent teacher, or to understand learning, or to be aware of the need for curriculum innovation, without a sound knowledge of education theory. But *I am* saying that we need to address these issues within SCL. To deny access to these intellectual concerns 'at the front door' means that they will only return unannounced elsewhere.

The SCL initiative quite rightly focuses attention upon the student experience, and the published aims and objectives make that explicit. My word of caution is that those of us who are engaged in the practice of education need to get 'our own house' in order along the way.

Not the least of the issues raised by SCL is that concerning the learning organisation. Now, in the context of H.E., this may seem tautological! However, in my experience, I am not so sure. To put it briefly (if only!), a learning organisation is 'where people continually expand their capacity to create results they truly desire, where new and expansive patterns of thinking are nurtured, where collective aspiration is set free, and where people are continually learning how to learn together.' (Senge, 1990).

So if we are to embrace SCL, we also have to consider this. This may encourage some people to suggest that this is another sound reason for doing nothing, but what might be the implications of taking such action? It is quite clear that complicated issues to do with our individual and collective identity are bound up in these concerns. Our own sense of self and self-esteem are central to our practice(s). Our sets of values are under threat, our workaday principles are under siege, and so on. And these are just the positive factors! To avoid being accused of sophistry, I would add that these issues do raise existential questions in that we know we should act, we feel that our actions are circumscribed by the contexts of our everyday lives, and to not act, or not act in harmony with our values would be to act in bad faith.

If we believe that our practice contributes to a learning organisation for our students, via the organisation of learning, do we also feel that this is true for ourselves? Are we as centred as we hope our students are, or will be?

We need to explicitly use theory and theorising to unpack SCL. Perhaps a good place to start would be to ask what we mean by: Student, Centred, and, Learning?

At this point I would just add a few thoughts, very much my own 'work in progress'.

What sort of student centred are we talking about? The autonomous individual (or even the individual seeking to be autonomous) ala reflexivity or flexible accumulation; *i.e.* the student in the singular?

Or, student in the plural: part of a community, where, among other things, the person's authority is derived from mutual inter-recognition and reciprocity? We are all free, action-taking/choice-making persons, social beings, in the sense of being part of the collective. We are not for oneself as much for ourselves, our life development is not just endlessly self-referential, but interrelated with others. We see ourselves through other's eyes, and constantly seek to 'remake' ourselves through these interfaces and interactions. For me this is an aspect of andragogy, the nature of adult learning and teaching related to adult needs. This raises questions like, is an adult education (in respect of learners and teachers) to be for liberation or domestication? While this may be a false dichotomy, *i.e.* nothing is ever that cut and dried, the issues are real enough.

In view of these basic questions, what do our educational, learning and teaching processes, encourage now? (*e.g.* via assessment?) What should we be encouraging? As practitioners we claim to deliver certain aspects of a curriculum (even broader educational goals as well), but what do we know of our effectiveness? If we (over) rely on the measurement of our efficacy by conventional techniques do we know whether our practice is effective, even efficient, in our own terms, or of others?

What do we understand by centred? Most contemporary wisdom suggests that the dominant human characteristic is a de-centredness, a demonstrable lack of self-actualisation, individually and/or collectively. This phenomena is variously called alienation, anomie, the saturated self; all suggesting that we are not fulfilling our potential, because we are trying to lead a life within an arrangement of networks, economic, social, cultural, moral, psychic, *etc.,* that actually prevents us from being fully human, really ourselves. And there is much, much more!

A good deal of the above comes back to a discussion of role and role interrelations. What do we inherit when we take on a role like student, or teacher, or learning supporter, or...? What is expected by us and by others? What is the nature of the relationships associated with these roles, *e.g.* power, trust, needs? What can we hope to achieve in this role and how does this relate to our identity, our sense of self and others, and others sense of us? Always bearing in mind, of course, that we are all multiple selves. Do we critically reflect upon relationships within, and with others as a constantly changing process, often set against a desire to achieve some degree of certainty, of continuity and security, in an uncertain, risky world?

135

Besides anything else, this can remind us that we are the subject of such reflection, and not objects that 'just get done to.' How self-consciously reflective and analytical we are will perhaps greatly influence the nature of our choices when faced with the bold reality of our freedom to take action: we have to do just that!

What then is the basis/motivations for our action/choice? Is it, are they, consistent, non-contradictory, in good faith, even virtuous? How would we know? Do we have a methodology to test this out? Is it explicit, 'on the table' for all to see?

Every so often we all see, and recognise, for what it is, the intersection of our own 'personal troubles' with the sets of social relations (including institutional ones) that are constantly changing in, and contextual to, our lives. Do we make key decisions about our significant transition at such points of intersection and revelation? Is this transformational in that we make qualitative leaps forward as such times to become the updated versions of ourselves, the people we want to be?

There is now an enormous literature on learning. Inevitably, a great deal of the literature is recycled. However, it is there, and a good deal of the key ideas have already been aired in the SCL initiative papers to date. It seems to me that one of our collective tasks is to clarify, and make some sense of, this extensive literature, demonstrating, as it does, the considerable twists and turns of theorising. A lot of these ideas are, as I have often said, more likely to clear the room, rather than clear the mind, but we do need to address these ideas.

One of the tricky questions is, do we keep all this theorising 'close to our chests', as the guardians of the knowledge, or do we engage with our students in making these ideas an aspect of the transparent process of education? Will they be grateful for our candour? Will they be empowered by becoming co-owners? And so on. Needless to say, these questions are part and parcel of the learning theory debate.

In a more practical way, how can we make this literature, this knowledge, these ideological debates and so on, accessible for everyone? I have already been discussing with colleagues the establishment of an 'archive' that would be as interactive as possible in that we would keep the materials up-to-date by using it as 'work in progress'. There are other means we need to discuss and develop.

We need to consider how to take the thinking about the SCL process forward. There is the SCL Week . . .and the Subject 'Awaydays', plus any other all-inclusive School, Depar-mental, or Faculty events. These various gatherings could be used to open up and widen dialogue.

In this very brief paper, I have attempted to set out a case for the value of theorisng at the heart of the SCL initiative. After all, this is a university.

REFERENCES
SENGE, PETER. *The Fifth Discipline; The Art and Practice of the Learning Organisation*, 1990.

Knowledge and Practice

(1992)

As identified earlier in this book (Bines, H. and Watson, D., eds., 1992), the conventional models of professional education in higher education are the technocratic and post-technocratic models. This, in turn, is part of increasingly practice-focused developments in professional education in many, if not most, professions at the moment, a factor which has much to do with the relative status given to 'academic' knowledge compared with 'practice knowledge'. The debates around the relative value of these knowledges is, in turn, the site of ideological struggles: which should be the more important in shaping the education of the practitioner? This case study will first discuss some general issues of knowledge and practice which have been the subject of debate at Oxford Polytechnic, and will then illustrate such issues with particular reference to the teaching of sociology on social work and health care courses.

One of the most significant aspects of such debates is the replacement of any single orthodoxy or conventional wisdom with another equally dominant one. There are also dangers in orienting education programmes to professional practice if the nature of the practice itself is not seen as problematic. Even where professions, or at least those associated with preparation for professions, are actively questioning the nature of knowledge, values and practice realities, they tend to overlook the problems of received ideas and conventional wisdoms. The professions that have developed even a broad range of motivations for practice, and where there are a variety of practice styles, still encourage the individual members of the profession to practice within an accepted and acceptable range. This has much to do with the current vogue for competence-related curriculum design.

One of our main aims in developing the concept of 'reflective practice' in education for professional practice is to challenge and question the nature of orthodoxies acting as social control. For example, one tendency in professional practice education has been for practitioners to consider their own and the profession's agenda before that of the client's, actual or potential. One of the paradoxes of professional education is that practitioners are encouraged to develop a critical awareness of the context of their practice, and the problems of their clients, while, at the same time, the notion is perpetuated that the professional practitioner is an autonomous, free-thinking agent.

Another dimension of professional education that has to be considered is exactly how do practitioners learn their practitioner role? If certain interventions are to be made into their conceptualisation of practice, we need to know how people do understand their role and see the conditions of their practice. (A similar point can be made about courses with less explicit vocational outcomes in that academics working on undergraduate courses intend to 'produce' able and insightful practitioners of that discipline or vocation. For example, biology staff aim to have able, competent biologists at the point of graduation and historians are similarly 'produced'.) So whether we explicitly put the question of 'practice' at the centre of the curriculum or not, that is where it is in reality in ensuing debates and arguments. A profession, or indeed, a discipline, not only has a practice; it also has a theory of action in which that practice can become reproducible, valid technique. This means that professional educators not only deal with questions of teaching technique to their students, but also in teaching the methods through which behavioural worlds can be created in which techniques can work. Our students thus need to know how to create the best environments for their practice. (Astley and Woolley, 1990).

However, how much of what we do as teachers is genuinely reflective in this sense? We are all theorists and our conceptual worlds contain theories-in-use, ideas about effective work practices which address questions like 'which approaches work well in particular contexts?' This involves us in seeking explanations about why they work well and leads us to a readiness to alter ways of working as dictated by recognisable changes in circumstances. Developing our theories-in-use acknowledges that contextual complexity of work-setting and problem-solving. These processes of critically reflecting on our actions also go beyond the cognitive into realms of artistry (Schön, 1983). They are intuitive, improvisational and creative. Indeed, much of what we produce is symbolic creativity in a very everyday way.

However, our own theories may well be somewhat different from, and perhaps come into conflict with, the espoused theories of our particular profession or educational hierarchy. Thus it is often the case that practitioners will claim to embrace the publicly espoused theories of their cultural grouping while actually continuing to practice according to their own criteria. Such espoused theories also often remain the unquestioned and unchallenged conventional wisdoms that practitioners may associate themselves within a very tortuous way. Conflicts such as these, therefore, need exposure and discussion, with the aims of reflection upon and improvements in our practice, and thereby our service to society. Considerations of these value orientations often focus on practical questions of who should teach what and where should this learning/teaching take place? One of the characteristics of a large number of professional education courses is that they borrow very heavily from other professions' bodies of specialist knowledge, such as the social or natural sciences. Indeed, the regulatory bodies for most professional education insist upon courses including such interventions into the curriculum. Part of the contradiction for these occupational groups is, therefore, that they argue for the need to include such knowledge in a professional course, a clear expression of the overlap of the technocratic and post-technocratic models of professional education, which may also represent a pragmatic response to changing knowledge status hierarchies.

The gradual upgrading of professional education, from certificate to diploma to degree for example, is seen as a positive step towards achieving full professional status. However, this raises unresolved questions about the relative status of knowledge bases that make up the curriculum, as well as the relative status of theory and practice. How can professions achieve their educational aims? Should they keep the specialist academic-bodies of knowledge in their courses, separately marked out in the curriculum, but taught by the host practitioners themselves, *i.e.* nurses, midwives or social workers who teach psychology or biology? This is certainly relevant when an increasing number of professional practitioners acquire degrees in 'academic' disciplines. Or should they get psychologists or biologists to teach (have real control over) these specialist bodies of knowledge? Even when such problems are resolved, how are these bodies of specialist knowledge to be taught? What needs to be learned and how? What decisions will be taken over appropriate learning environments and who will have the final say over assessment? This involves questions about similarities and differences between courses and whether they are epistemological, functional to the particular course or social, in terms of the organisation of the knowledge/discipline group. It also raises questions about the relationships between research and practice, the relative status of 'academic' and 'professional' knowledge and the social relationships between the various staff involved.

Issues of knowledge (and power) relationships between staff and students are also pertinent. In a formalised professional education context (as discussed by Bines, above) it is also essential for the educator to take into consideration the debate on learning and cognitive styles. The 'reflective practitioner' should give due consideration to the ways in which interaction between teachers and learners takes place. Such questions are relevant both to the role of the academic specialists, those who are not members of the profession in question, and that of the professional practitioners themselves. Whether the aim is to introduce students to new skills, tasks or ideas, or to advance or develop the skills of existing practitioners, we also need to consider in what ways such things become less part of the teacher and more part of the student. Lying behind such concerns is the possibility of the imposition of a body of cultural and professionally sanctified knowledge and practice, particularly in a predetermined curriculum delivered regardless of the existing status, knowledge and experience of students. Our orientation could be different if we started from the premise that people of varying status in these professional education situations already know and do a great deal. They may have quite well-developed ideas of their own or as a group about what they want to do and how they feel is the best way to do it. Drawing on Knowles (1973) and others, do we adequately recognise the active role of adult learners in the processes of 'their' education?

KNOWLEDGE AND PRACTICE IN PROFESSIONAL COURSES AT OXFORD POLYTECHNIC

As noted elsewhere in this book, lecturers who are primarily teachers of 'academic disciplines' make a number of contributions to professional courses. Life scientists, for example, teach on most of the health care courses while sociologists contribute to courses ranging from social work to management education. In each of these courses, aims include the teaching of relevant aspects of the discipline to support students' developing professional knowledge and action.

Such inputs may be made in a variety of ways although they are increasingly being integrated into professional elements of courses. In the new Diploma in Social Work, for example, some formerly discrete elements of the social sciences, such as law, psychology, sociology and social policy, are largely integrated into modules that are based on the issues, principles and practices of social work. This could be seen to reflect a largely functional view of the role of social science in social work education, together with sociology's epistemological concerns with the nature of society and social institutions that are also a focus of social work practice. A similar approach is found in health care courses. In addition, other aspects of a discipline may have an impact on why and how it is taught. Sociology, as a critical and reflexive discipline, not only offers a particular approach to substantive topics, such as the family or health, but also has considerable potential in relation to the critical analysis of professional practice itself. It thus can play a special role in tackling some of the issues raised earlier, such as the relationship between knowledge and practice, the espoused theories of a particular profession and social relationships between professionals and clients.

The sociological debate around professionals' discretionary power is particularly interesting in this respect. In my experience, a good majority of social work students have very mixed feelings about 'having' and 'using' power. They would like to be optimistic about their use of power but they have doubts. A reflexive sociological approach to such issues can do much to elaborate such concerns and offer potential bases for both beliefs and practice.

Sociology can also be related to the developing professional role in the 'practicum'. In relation to critical examination of knowledge and practice, any teachers organising and facilitating courses for professional practitioners are, or should be, engaged in creating 'models of practice'. This is done via theory and debates around bodies of knowledge appropriate to the practice in question, linked to some form of work or practice experience for the students to try out their skills, reflect on the theories espoused and be

143

coached in the techniques and arts of practice. Teaching sociology on a social work course should reflect such principles. For example, it does not take long before students are asked, 'what is the nature of the social on which you are working?' They may well respond in terms of the received ideas of their practice, in particular some form of pathological model of society or individualised human behaviour. However, the aim is not to make the students feel foolish or inadequate, but on the contrary to debate the conventions of their practice culture and suggest that a sociological perspective might seek to challenge assumptions, including, of course, the value of specialised knowledge included in the course! Certainly, this is social control, but it has the positive dimensions of the desire to create the necessary overall learning environment of 'practicum'. One key aspect of this is to recognise that debates about theories and received ideas taking place in the classroom or the laboratory are just as much part of this overall learning environment as anything else, and that part of the skill in designing and facilitating a course is to get the balance right. This may not be easy, especially if students are not convinced, via their own experience, of the relevance and interdependency of the different aspects, and often requires reflective and innovative approaches to teaching and learning.

As noted above, such relationships between knowledge and practice inevitably raise issues about the relationships between academic and professional knowledge, research and practice, and staff and students, including the role of the adult learner. Certainly. my experience of 'mature' students on nursing and social work courses confirms the general pattern that such students may feel de-(life) skilled in general and experience bouts of doubt about the relevance of their past occupational practice. They can acquire the impression that by and large their previous experience is to be left at the classroom door and that this is an inevitable part of the teaching/learning contract. Thus any sociology (or other) curriculum needs to begin with an ack-nowledgement of students' existing knowledge, skills and experience. In the teaching of sociology, this will include acknowledgements of their existing skills and experience in managing the self and the social, and the set of theories that students may hold as a consequence of such processes. Learning strategies are designed to draw out such theories, while comparing and contrasting them to the range of sociological theories on offer. Students then not only have the opportunity to reflect on their own theories of action, seeing them for what they are, but can also make judgements about the relative values to be placed on other theories, without denying themselves as skilled social actors, or the possibilities for change.

Nevertheless, even with such an open and reflective approach to adult learners, and to the relationship between knowledge and practice, it can still be difficult to develop particular forms of learning, teaching and assessment. For example, in relation to the use of essays as part of assessed course work in social work and post-registration nursing courses, it is not easy to persuade students to reflect on, write about and reflect upon again, their practice experience. There appear to be two main explanations for this. Firstly, students are concerned lest they should fail to comply with the 'academic' expectations of their course, since personal life, educational or work experience has taught them to devalue their own observations and assessment of the world. They also find it difficult to integrate a reflective evaluation of their own practice into the conventional essay mode of exposition. Course design must, therefore, focus on es-tablishing a learning and teaching framework which fac-ilitates a range of routes to knowledge and to data.

Relationships between knowledge, practice, students and staff are also reflected in debates about research. This can be illustrated by discussion on the developments of the nursing and midwifery degrees, the Diploma in Nursing, and

145

the new Diploma in Social Work. There was resistance in all three cases to including a 'research module'. In two instances, it was the nurse practitioners who wanted to introduce the element of research early on in the courses, which was resisted as unnecessary by some life scientists, who felt that the research element in their contributory disciplines was sufficient. In contrast, in the social work case, it was the social scientists who argued the need to establish some clear research guidelines for the course, giving rise to mixed reactions from the social work practitioners, some of whom felt this was not really a necessary set of issues or skills. The link in all three instances was the establishment of specialist professional knowledge together with the clear commitment of the protagonists for a curriculum ideology that 'came clean' with students about the nature of knowledge.

However, despite such tensions, discipline-based and profession-based staff can successfully collaborate on courses for the professions. Such collaboration, however, requires a particular view of the role of the academic specialist. They should be valuable not merely because of their specialist knowledge base, but because of the relationship between that knowledge base and their practice as a teacher. An experienced teacher of a natural or social science, with a highly sensitised orientation and commitment to the practice and education of other professions, may, justifiably, be a member of a professional education team, particularly since this then avoids the segmented delivery of bodies of knowledge assumed to be relevant to professional practice in favour of a reflective practice which includes the content, teaching and learning of the course itself. The teaching of sociology in professional courses at Oxford Polytechnic does attempt to reflect both the broad and reflexive role of the discipline and such aspirations in relation to the role of the teacher. Although this may, as yet, be difficult to fully implement in practice across all disciplines and in all professional courses, debates on such issues are beginning to create the conditions for future realisation.

Conclusion

A sociological perspective on all the above suggests that we are actually discussing the 'interaction order' of education for professional practice of whatever kind. Human beings, with all their public and private diversity and homogeneity, are being assessed as members of a professional/ occupational culture. Issues of selfhood and social accountability are fairly clear. A consideration of the conditions of our practice is not an 'out there' abstract activity. As teachers and researchers engaged in the design, delivery, assessment and evaluation of courses for professional practitioners, we are also required to spend a significant amount of time and energy considering the processes of these educational programmes as well as the product.

REFERENCES
ASTLEY, J. and WOOLLEY, T. 'Reflecting on the interface between learning and teching'. *Teaching News*, 26, Autumn, Oxford Polytechnic, 1990
BINES, H. and WATSON, D. (eds.). *Developing Professional Education*, Open University Press, Buckingham, 1992
KNOWLES, M. *The Adult Learner; A Forgotten Species.* Croom Helm, London, 1973
SCHÖN, D. A. *The Reflective Practitioner.* Temple Smith, London, 1983

The Quest for the Good Community

(1997)

Throughout the opening weeks of 1997, the pages of *Community Care* were filled even more than usual with arguments about the moral climate in contemporary society. It is true that considerable attention to these concerns has also been regularly aired in *The Guardian* and other journals of middle class discourse. The impending General Election might also have had something to do with these discussions. Given the name and main aims of *Community Care*, its focus on professional practice and social policy issues, the airing of philosophical concerns such as the 'moral climate' was neither a surprising nor unwelcome development. The combination of articles and news items represented opinion and reflected concern about the state of people and their social relationships in Britain today, and offered a commentary, even a guide through the issues, the moral maze.

Several of the writers commented on the Conservative Government's (and politicians in general) cynical disregard for any version of truth other than their own. People working with a different set of values from those 'in power' are understandably angry and even frustrated. What is of great concern to many, of course, is not just their frustration with the 'product' of social administration, but also with the process. Those of us involved in social care and welfare have no special rights or privileges in regard to dismay and disappointment. Nor can we always claim that the set of values which help direct and inform our practice are not shared by other citizens. But we can and do often argue that our day-to-day involvement in the organisation and delivery of welfare and care gives us an insight into the trials and tribulations of 'The Community'. Is there anybody out there? Is anyone in authority actually listening, taking any notice of what we say and do? Are we, even, occasionally bothered by that little voice that suggests that, 'the great British public' are greedy, selfish and self-interested, always open to some cut price, 'knock 'em down and drag them out' political rhetoric? As a Woody Allen character once said, 'It's not just dog eat dog in this town, it's dog doesn't even return dog's phone calls!'

In short, I feel we are often caught between what Karl Mannheim called 'Ideology and Utopia'; the fictions that crowd into our information gathering scope on the one hand and the wish dreams that we still hold to and aim to realise one day. There is no doubt that the pages of *Community Care* are part of the discourses, the processes of argument and debate, which impinge on our lives and work. It hardly seems necessary to engage further with discussion about the ideology bit, other than to reconfirm my belief that the 'meeting point' of argument about ideas and values is part of the process of identification for us, part of the way we relate our sense of self to that constant unravelling of the day-to-day realities of life.

I want to focus attention on the utopia bit. In particular, I want to consider how the concept and conceptualising of Community is, for many of us, a crucial aspect of our lives.

I would argue that most 'people workers' engaged in social care and welfare are 'walking reservoirs' of ideas on community. We do share a common vision that 'the good community' does exist, has existed, can exist. We share the belief that the quest for the 'good community' is a worthy, even heroic one. Most of us wear this set of values 'on our sleeves', constantly open to the elements and the impact of the hurly-burly of everyday life. Constant repairs are needed to keep everything workable and we regularly draw deeply on our reserves. Relevant to these ideas about 'the good community', these reserves are, I feel, made up of three key parts.

Firstly, there is the community as fact; our understanding and assessment of how things are at the moment; the good, the bad and the ugly. It is here, in part, that we rely on accurate information, on the dissemination of current research, on evaluation and assessment of innovative practice, and so on.

Secondly, there is community as ideal; this is largely the utopia bit, what we feel life ought to be like. It is here that we draw on a complex diversity of ideas, values, emotions, interpretations and understandings of the/our/their pasts, wish dreams, and so on. Into this 'ideological melting pot' has probably also gone aspects of our professional education, our youthful enthusiasms and idealism, and our mature and wise reflection.

Thirdly, there is community as practice, and practise. It is my reading of contemporary life that many/most people feel alienated, and with good reason. It is not a novel idea to suggest that creativity can be an antidote to alienation. This 'creativity' involves taking charge of processes, using resources to pose and express alternatives to the usual diet of selfishness and mediocrity. We must, in all good reason, put morality back onto a footing which enables a genuinely open debate about social needs, personal troubles and a 'commonwealth'.

What I see around me all the time, and read about at length, is that many people, professional practitioners and otherwise, are practicing/practising their way out of the current malaise, resisting the pious humbug and political myopia, and working towards the 'good community'. What does concern me greatly is the continued sense of isolation that many people feel. Contemporary life has a way of fragmenting ourselves, of throwing into doubt the values and beliefs we have nourished. What needs to be done with some urgency is to reinvest people with a sense of collective commitments to the quest for the good community. It is true, of course, that a couple of years ago there was a brief excursion down this road by Blair and Co. in response to some rehashed ideas on 'Communitas' by Etzioni and the like. But that was yesterday's sound bite, and the 'ownership' of that engagement, did not get far beyond Westminster or Academia. A lasting commitment to the quest for the good community needs to come from those at the 'grassroots', who really do have a vested interest in both the idea and the actuality of social change.

One of the key issues here is the relationship between membership of a culture group and the process of identification that shapes our identity. Identity sounds very fixed, as if the question of having an identity is clear-cut and unchanging. What is more likely is that we are always engaged in the development of 'our' identity, even, for example, spending some time in both maintaining and protecting it, but without doubt, our identities can be under threat!

Membership of a culture group plays an important part in this process of taking on and having an identity. We do need to identify with significant others, ideas, values, lifestyles and so on, and this makes up what is usually seen as the process of identification. John Shotter's notion of 'the self and social accountability' might be helpful here; Shotter argues that we constantly seek reinforcement and legitimation from others that we are 'getting it right', satisfactorily being a human being.

One of the key issues to be addressed here is the nature of Organisations. We need to consider the complexity of their cultures in relation to practice.

Let me start by reiterating that organisations are people and the sets of relationships that they have with other people. Internal relations contribute a large part to what constitutes any organisation's culture, its way of life, replete, of course, with considerable symbolism. The relations that members of an organisation have with 'outsiders' is also crucial in understanding the nature of the organisation. A good deal of an organisation's symbolic activity is invested into creating and maintaining boundaries, separating this 'community' from that. When we think about organisations, especially perhaps ones that we are regularly involved with, it is important to remind ourselves that we are not just thinking about and describing what people do, role performance and the like, but what meanings they and we place upon what they do. How conscious, indeed self-conscious, are we? I am not going to argue here that it is only professional practitioners in the 'people industries' that take issue with their practice, are reflective about it, and so on. Nor do I want to suggest that it is easy for us to focus clearly on the tangled relations that make up our practice 'within' the context of the organisation. But deal with these complexities we must, because in a state of constant and far-reaching change, including a fragmentation of conventional modes of practice and its organisation, even if we do not investigate these matters, other people will be. These other people are very likely to be those that manage us in one way or another.

Practice is very much to do with ideas, and the development of these ideas is a dialectical process. We hold to a thesis, other ideas emerge from all manner of sources including ourselves (an aspect of being reflective and research minded practitioners), this is anti-thesis.

Out of the ensuing 'struggle' of reason and desire comes a new synthesis, a paradigm of practice knowledge: for example, from which we work, and so the process of change goes on. However, change is also about alienation; it is bound up with our feelings of powerlessness, of loss of control over the process of change. We, individually and collectively, have invested heavily in our practice, we retain ideas about autonomy and choice, about the best judgments based on a set of values that reflects giving service to society. But we do not have complete ownership of either organisational cultures or the process of change. It is also obvious that our practice, and changes to it, is not just a set of ideas; it does have a material - real people, real lives, resources, *etc.* - basis to it. It is also necessary to remind ourselves that, through our continued role performance as professional practitioners we are inextricably part of the processes of the organisational culture. We cannot 'have our cake and eat it'; we cannot disclaim responsibility for change, we are an essential part of it. To look change in the face and argue that this is nothing to do with us is an example of what C. Wright Mills called 'crackpot realism' and what some psychologists might call cognitive dissonance. We know that we are wrong, but don't intend to let that stand in our way, especially from disowning change on the basis that 'it is nothing to do with us'.

In this brief paper I have considered some issues which, for me at least, are central to practice and practise. The questions of values is never far away, and these fundamental aspects of our motivation for action need regular scrutiny in our Quest for the Good Community.

REFERENCES

ETZIONI, A. *The Community of Spirit*, 1993
MANNHEIM, K. *Ideology and Utopia*, 1936
MILLS, C. WRIGHT. *The Sociological Imagination*, 1959
SHOTTER, J. *Social Accountability and Selfhood*, 1984

This paper was given to a seminar of colleagues at Reading University in 1997.